The Four Gates

READER COMMENTS

In the royal realm of reality there are four gates. As we progress into the realm we discover that each gate is an indispensable, direct means to fulfillment, but none is sufficient in itself. You learn about your true Self, but knowledge is not enough. You learn to experience your essence and cultivate behaviors congruent to yourself, but this also is not enough. You learn love and devotion to the Being you really are, and even then, something more is required for the life you long for. As the tale masterfully unfolds, you discover the complete path to living in clarity, self-awareness and real fulfillment. You, the reader, are the participant in this saga!
- P.R. Realtor

The Four Gates offers so many layers of knowledge with such clarity that it evokes in the sincerely focused reader the experience of the path to real fulfillment in life. With every reading an even more profound experience is available.
- M.M. Life Coach

C. S. Lewis said the gates of hell are locked from the inside. In *The Four Gates*, Dr. Erhard Vogel shows us how to find the key, and then draws a map and personally guides us out of pain and suffering into the royal realm to claim our place in it. In these pages the sincere wanderer is provided step-by-step instruction to limitless self-experience and self-expression.
- J.B. Realtor

The Four Gates is a masterful guide to personal development. The story subtly and powerfully takes us on a journey of self-discovery and shows us the true path to fulfillment. An easy-to-follow and important book that is bound to change lives.
- J.S. Realtor

From the beginning of this tale, the author helps you establish a positive and real foundation for self-experience, which makes it

possible to accomplish this vitally important inner journey with enjoyment, ease and ever-increasing self-trust. As you read, you are personally guided safely, lovingly and expertly. The self-development afforded by *The Four Gates* is a truly remarkable accomplishment, both by the author and by the sincere reader.
- M.K. Music Teacher

The Four Gates is a beautiful and inspiring tale. It is also so much more. It is a practical guide to experiencing a fulfilling life. Any questions you may ask, and any questions you don't ask, are answered. Read this book!
- F.S. Elementary School Teacher

This book expresses the journey to fulfillment. It is, by far, one of the greatest works I have read. As I engage in it and apply its insights, I can see the profound changes it makes in how I relate to my family, my community and, most importantly, to myself. If you are sincere in your life's journey, this book will be an invaluable guide to reaching fulfillment in Self-realization.
- Dr. R.T.

I love the format the author has chosen to write in. I find myself reading and evolving as I identify with the wanderer and absorb the experience. There is nothing in the saga that I cannot agree with and have found myself continually saying, 'I know this to be true.' As I continue in my reading, I expand in consciousness from wanderer to aspirant, and I am hungry for more. I am living it!
- B.L. Realtor

READER COMMENTS

In the royal realm of reality there are four gates. As we progress into the realm we discover that each gate is an indispensable, direct means to fulfillment, but none is sufficient in itself. You learn about your true Self, but knowledge is not enough. You learn to experience your essence and cultivate behaviors congruent to yourself, but this also is not enough. You learn love and devotion to the Being you really are, and even then, something more is required for the life you long for. As the tale masterfully unfolds, you discover the complete path to living in clarity, self-awareness and real fulfillment. You, the reader, are the participant in this saga!
- P.R. Realtor

The Four Gates offers so many layers of knowledge with such clarity that it evokes in the sincerely focused reader the experience of the path to real fulfillment in life. With every reading an even more profound experience is available.
- M.M. Life Coach

C. S. Lewis said the gates of hell are locked from the inside. In *The Four Gates*, Dr. Erhard Vogel shows us how to find the key, and then draws a map and personally guides us out of pain and suffering into the royal realm to claim our place in it. In these pages the sincere wanderer is provided step-by-step instruction to limitless self-experience and self-expression.
- J.B. Realtor

The Four Gates is a masterful guide to personal development. The story subtly and powerfully takes us on a journey of self-discovery and shows us the true path to fulfillment. An easy-to-follow and important book that is bound to change lives.
- J.S. Realtor

From the beginning of this tale, the author helps you establish a positive and real foundation for self-experience, which makes it

possible to accomplish this vitally important inner journey with enjoyment, ease and ever-increasing self-trust. As you read, you are personally guided safely, lovingly and expertly. The self-development afforded by *The Four Gates* is a truly remarkable accomplishment, both by the author and by the sincere reader.
- M.K. Music Teacher

The Four Gates is a beautiful and inspiring tale. It is also so much more. It is a practical guide to experiencing a fulfilling life. Any questions you may ask, and any questions you don't ask, are answered. Read this book!
- F.S. Elementary School Teacher

This book expresses the journey to fulfillment. It is, by far, one of the greatest works I have read. As I engage in it and apply its insights, I can see the profound changes it makes in how I relate to my family, my community and, most importantly, to myself. If you are sincere in your life's journey, this book will be an invaluable guide to reaching fulfillment in Self-realization.
- Dr. R.T.

I love the format the author has chosen to write in. I find myself reading and evolving as I identify with the wanderer and absorb the experience. There is nothing in the saga that I cannot agree with and have found myself continually saying, 'I know this to be true.' As I continue in my reading, I expand in consciousness from wanderer to aspirant, and I am hungry for more. I am living it!
- B.L. Realtor

ALSO BY ERHARD VOGEL

Books:

*A Dialogue With Death The Teacher Of Life
An Ancient Story For The Modern World*

Journey Into Your Center

Self-Healing Through the Awareness of Being (out of print)

Audio Publications of Guided Meditations and Teachings:

The Cave Meditation

The Stress Release Response: 7 Steps to Triumph Over Stress

Guided Meditation for Beginners

Centering

Feelings and Emotions

The Healing Power of Love

The Silent Observer

Yoga for Life: Two Hours of Guided Yoga Classes Advanced

Breathing Techniques and the Breath Meditation

Please see back of the book for descriptions of audio publications.

The Four Gates

A Saga Of The Human Being On The Path
From The Pit of Despair To The Realm Of Fulfillment,
From Confusion To Clarity,
Culminating In The Deepest Realization

Erhard Vogel

The Four Gates is derived from a spontaneous talk
given by Dr. Erhard Vogel at the Nataraja Yoga Ashram in 1986, in
honor of visiting sage H.H. Swami Chidanandaji.

Nataraja Ashram
San Diego, California

Books may be ordered through booksellers or by contacting:
Nataraja Yoga Ashram
10171 Hawley Road
El Cajon, California 92021
info@yogameditationnataraja.org

ISBN: 978-1-892484-09-3 (sc)
ISBN: 978-1-892484-10-9 (e)

Library of Congress Control Number: 2015911778

DEDICATION

This book is dedicated
to those who share the light of reality,
teachers and students alike,
and contribute to the cessation of suffering,
thereby making a difference with their lives
and leaving a positive mark on humanity.

IN GRATITUDE

I thank the luminous Himalayan sages H.H. Swami Krishnanandaji and H.H. Swami Chidanandaji for being such steady and devoted examples of life experienced in the joy of Being and for their loving friendships that have so enriched my life; the staff of the Nataraja Yoga Ashram for their devotion in managing the workings of the Ashram; Kathleen McMillen for her thorough and devoted editing and formatting of the manuscript; and my students for their sincere endeavors in making lasting positive change within themselves and humanity.

CONTENTS

DEAR READER

This story includes detailed points of
knowledge that guide you on the path to
fulfillment through living according to
your true identity and thereby freeing yourself from the self-imposed
limitations that curtail human lives.

Please read in a way by which you experience and savor this
knowledge that has been an integral part of the human experience for
ages. Allow the experience to sink in and become part of you. Thus
you will accomplish a deep-reaching transformation within yourself.
Follow the loving guidance offered and evolve along with the wanderer
to your final fulfillment. The story of the wanderer is the story of each
one of us.

To help you establish an intimate connection with this human
representative, I have chosen to transcend the gender issue by
alternately referring to the wanderer as 'she' and 'he.' It is my hope
that you will soon become used to this practice and be in touch with
the masculine and feminine aspects that serve us all.

One more consideration:

This story is for the reader who sincerely wants to learn and grow.
What is written here is not difficult to understand, because it is about
you and innate to you. Reading with sincerity, patience and care while

you *experience* yourself as the wanderer, will have you grow into an understanding of yourself that will fill you with love, joy and the expertise of being truly you.

Regarding the use of language: Words are beautiful means of clarifying the world—including our ideas, thoughts and feelings—to each other and, especially, to ourselves. I aim to represent the beauty and strength of truth with words that do it full justice and stimulate growth—not only in the use of language, but also in the ability to experience on subtler and more expansive levels.

However, the challenge lies not in the words—most of us know the words used here—but in the way they are applied: in a thoroughly focused mode. Experiencing the meaning these words convey stimulates a steady growth of focus in your mind. Do you not want that?

Now, just a few brief technical notes:

'Being' with a capital 'B' represents all that is being; 'being' with a lower case 'b' represents the being that Being does.

The word 'Self' denotes the real identity as differentiated from 'self,' the false ego identity.

In the special framed teachings, nouns are capitalized for emphasis.

Additionally, see the Glossary of Terms at the end of the book.

By the way, I sincerely invite you to share your responses to the ideas in this book by emailing me at info@yogameditationnataraja.org

A WORD TO
THE WISE

This saga is devoted to helping
your evolution to the highest levels of consciousness.

Read to experience; focus on living the knowledge offered here.

FOCUS

Absorb yourself now in full and continuous focus
as a sincere person on the path of life.

Flow in accord with the universal flow.
Guide your faculties—
your mind, feelings, emotions, senses,
intellect and intuition—
to your center, the area of your heart.
Cause them to be present to yourself in harmonious balance,
deeply at ease,
feeling at home,
in comfort and security.

Your center is one limitless field of consciousness;
let it be entirely clear and uncluttered.
Cause your faculties to rest in consciousness,
to be receptive and deeply engaged
in the experience I am about to share with you...

FINDING THE ROYAL REALM

Most of us share in the same dilemma:
>   we suffer from falsity and fear
>   in the perception of ourselves as limited and lacking,
>   while deep within us stirs the knowledge of our heritage
>   and our destiny,
>   of our interconnectedness
>   and our potential for fulfillment.

All about us is evidence of life in separateness,
>   of waiting, wanting and yearning,
>   of needing and desiring,
>   of pain and sorrow,
>   a life of deep-seated turmoil
>   in which we feel afflicted
>   by the lack of direction and decisiveness:
>   a life of suffering.

You may say that you do not want such a life.
>   Do you, perhaps, have the good fortune
>   to know *what* you want—
>   what you really want?

To know what you really want,
>   you must know who you essentially are,

for how can you be fulfilled in yourself
if you do not know who you are?
The knowledge of your real identity we will explore.

Some like to be exposed to knowledge in fictional terms—
clothed in a story—
and some like to have only the plain facts.
So I shall tell you a story of fact,
a children's story for adults.

Again, I invite you to relax and enjoy,
focused and present in the Being that you are.
Savor and absorb this story.
Keep your mind clear;
cause it to be like a tranquil mountain lake,
able to absorb and reflect without distortion
all the knowledge regarding the Self that you are.
Open yourself to the experience of your history
and your destiny.

Once upon all time,
there is a person who lives in a most miserable world.

Experience yourself as this person.

The place is barren and dreary;
it feels cold and damp to the bone
and is filled with odors of putrefaction,
dank and foul.
The sounds are dissonant and painful to the ear.

The sky is always gray,
as is the land.
You can barely distinguish a horizon in the murky atmosphere;
all is one vague muddiness.

Allow yourself to feel *the world in which this person lives.*

Nothing gives comfort here;
nothing feels good or pleasurable.

The person dwelling here feels deeply unhappy.
She wanders about day in and day out,
not knowing where to go or what to do
or how to attain relief from the discomfort and anxiety
she perpetually suffers.
She desperately attempts to survive
in the lifeless, thoroughly depressing place.
After all, this is where she has dwelled
for as long as she can remember.

So he wanders around and around in the barren land,
until one day he cannot go any further:
he has fallen into a deep pit of despair.
No longer can he wander aimlessly.
He feels frozen in exhaustion,
arrested in depression;
his drive to move on is depleted.
He finds himself severely limited, restricted;

it seems as if all his options have been eliminated.

There is nowhere to go.

He endeavors to climb out of the pit
> by making little attempts here and there.
> But each passing feint at escape consumes more of his energy,
> energy he already desperately lacks.
> Eventually he loses all hope
> of ever freeing himself from this painful situation.
> He feels too depressed to even hope.

Yet he still struggles,
> gnashing his teeth with despair and frustration.
> He knows not what to do.
> Throughout his life he has looked for improvement,
> yearned for peace and vitality,
> for relief from the deeply depressing monotony.

Allow yourself to feel this.

She has looked for clarity throughout her life
> but found none;
> all she ever found was a thick fog limiting her view.

Now, whenever she takes a few steps in this direction or that,
> she meets obstacles and boundaries,
> the walls of the pit.
> No matter what she tries,
> she never seems to succeed.

She becomes deeply frustrated, disheartened,
hopelessly trapped in the deep pit of despair.

Somehow, though, she knows
> that the world of despair in which she lives
> has always been alien to her.
> It has never really been her home,
> even though she has lived here longer than she can remember.
> And now, strangely, she notices that she is homesick;
> she yearns for her real home.

She has always known she could never be happy here
> but never knew what to do about it.
> Now she is stuck in this terrible pit.
> Filled with anger and fear,
> trembling with anxiety,
> she struggles with even greater desperation and tenacity
> to claw herself out of the pit of despair.

One day, as he struggles to climb out,
> just when things seem most hopeless,
> over the edge of the pit he catches a glimpse
> of something in the distance,
> radiantly beautiful and rich,
> promising joy and fulfillment.
> He has a brief but deep-reaching experience
> of an entirely different world.

He experiences a suggestion of clarity.

> He feels the promise of freedom.
>
> That realm appears luminous,
>
> resplendent with all the colors of the rainbow.
>
> The atmosphere is clear and nurturing,
>
> soothing, loving, warm.
>
> It seems gentle and luxuriant, vibrant with fresh life.

He is flooded with such a wealth of heart-stirring experience

> in that brief but potent moment
>
> that it leaves an indelible impression upon him.

That one glimpse of the wonderful world is compelling enough

> to inspire in him great determination and focus
>
> to cease his habitual struggle,
>
> to let go.
>
> He delivers himself out of the pit.

Once out of the pit

> she starts walking with resolve
>
> on a direct path toward the luminous domain
>
> that is now her focal point.
>
> As she consciously directs her actions to take her there,
>
> she keeps the sight of the beautiful realm
>
> in the forefront of her memory.
>
> This gives her the energy to persevere.

You see, she has lived in despair for so long,

> she has suffered so abjectly in the land of murk,

that she knows now,

no matter how long she stays in this barren land,

no matter what she tries,

no matter how far she meanders in the grayness,

she will never, never, never find happiness here.

The wanderer is completely determined now;

whatever it takes,

even if it is her last ounce of strength and her last breath,

she will reach the realm of luminous joy.

To remain in the land of suffering

offers no advantage whatsoever.

She proceeds with pure resolve.

Finally about to leave her past of misery behind,

she reaches the border of the resplendent realm.

Then something strange occurs within her.

She hesitates.

She stops.

Feel yourself standing at the border of the luminous realm,

about to leave your past behind.

He is filled with fear again.

Now he fears giving up the dark world of suffering

he has always considered his home.

He fears leaving behind the possessions, places

and painful experiences

that are part of the dreary world.

He fears letting go of his fears.
He fears letting go of his fears!

He has lost his vitality,
    the joyous energy he experienced
    when drawn to the realm of light and color.
    He does not remember the frustration and pain,
    the loneliness and anguish
    he suffered in the land of darkness.
    As he now stops in front of the realm of solace
    with all its color and infinite promise,
    he fears to let go of the world of anguish.
    He has forgotten that this barren place will never benefit him.

In this strange turn of events,
    the wanderer attempts to deceive himself with the illusion
    that he is attracted to the *familiarity* of the lifeless land
    in which he has endured so much suffering.
    He expends his energy in imagination and rationalization
    attempting to brighten the desolate place,
    imbuing it with the colors of the alluring realm
    that he had glimpsed in the distance
    when he was in the pit.

After a while, he recognizes
    that painting the drab world with illusory colors
    does not work.
    This cannot work.
    It will never work.

No matter how hard he tries to deceive himself
that the dreary place has color, vitality and pleasure,
he knows he can never achieve the satisfaction here
that is so clearly promised
in the realm beckoning him with its real bounty and color.

And yet he is so absorbed in his attachment to the lifeless world,
it feels like he is leaving his home,
even though he knows it is a prison
and not his home.

So she struggles.
She feels bound to the domain of despair
while deeply pulled to the realm of fulfillment.

To free herself from the paralysis caused by this struggle,
she makes a conscious decision to override the false urges
that bind her to the familiar misery.
She discovers within herself the ability
to let go of attachment to lack and suffering.
Summoning her determination,
her honesty, integrity, commitment
and the strength she feels growing within,
she tears herself free from the ties
binding her to the world of despondency.

Now she perceives that the illusory processes within—
automatic ways of thinking and feeling
rooted in her bleak past—

produced her attachment to the depressing land.
To continue in this attachment is sheer absurdity.

The wanderer renews her determination with strengthened sincerity.
With a sense of purpose she directs herself again
toward the real splendor,
the color, light and clarity
of the promising realm that beckons.
She focuses all her efforts to be present,
to realistically assess what is
and what she really wants.

Again she finds herself standing at the border of the radiant realm
that caught her eye so long ago.
The beauty of this realm had inspired her hopes
and given her the energy to struggle out of the pit of despair
and come to this point.

Her inner perception has shifted, subtly but powerfully.
She chooses to no longer allow her attachment to the past
to deceive her;
her attraction to this new life is real.
She frees herself from the destructive, self-limiting attachment
to the oppressive world
and is greeted by the full promise before her:
light, vitality, satisfaction and joy.

Now she meets a new problem:
How do I enter?

Again he wanders about,

> confused and frightened, fatigued and discouraged.
> And yet he determines to follow his inspiration,
> no matter how daunting the challenges.

Thus, one day,

> when he is especially sincere and clear,
> he discovers a great portal—
> the entrance to the resplendent realm.
> He rushes forward, but he is stymied again:
> he knows not how to open it.

He determines to solve this puzzle.

> In order to discover the solution,
> his mind has to be clear and calm.
> To achieve that state, he disciplines his mind
> by tenaciously keeping it focused
> on the puzzle of how to enter.
> He purposefully engages in great austerities
> that strengthen his mind's ability to focus.

And lo, at last,

> the door to the luminous realm is flung open,
> and there stands a magnificent figure,
> a radiant Being.

The wanderer is immediately aware of the absolute kindness,

> the benevolence of this Being who stands at the open entrance.
> He realizes with clarity and immense astonishment,

he is in the presence of the king of the realm!
This he *knows* without doubt.

The king gazes upon the wanderer gently,
> with love and kindness,
> and welcomes him to the home of lasting fulfillment:
> Come within.

How do I enter?

And the king says unto him,
> The moment you decide to be ready, oh wanderer,
> truly ready,
> you will be able to enter this realm.

The wanderer has suffered so long in the arid wasteland
> that he is taken aback by the king's simple invitation
> to enter the realm of fulfillment.
> And yet it fills his heart with elation,
> a joy he has never known before
> and has always sought.

The king disappears from her sight.

Left alone, the wanderer assesses herself
> and resolves strongly to acknowledge her innermost drives
> toward her deepest satisfaction.
> She realizes that her yearnings and inspirations,
> her desires, ambitions and even instincts
> throughout her life in the land of misery
> were to be here in this beautiful realm.

Even though *she* did not know it,
her *heart* knew.

She determines to honor these inspirations and drives
and to overcome her hesitancy,
as she now attempts to go into the realm of fulfillment.
She walks a few steps toward the entrance
and meets an invisible barrier that stops her progress.
Once again, she does not know what to do.

The wanderer says to herself,
I let go of my attachment to the bleak place of the past,
I overcame my hesitancy and made my determination,
I am right here at the entrance,
but this invisible obstacle is holding me back.

She is able to look into the realm of abundance
and catch glimpses of recognition.
There is something enduring there,
something substantial,
something real.
She sees people dwelling there,
people of luminous beauty and grace.
They are full of exuberance,
moving freely,
deeply fulfilled in their beauty
and the abundance of their realm.
They engage fully with whatever their hearts desire.

Our wanderer aspires

      to be like these indwellers of the delightful realm.

      She wants to be there.

      But she is stuck, truly stuck now,

      and she feels the pain of being outside,

      of being isolated.

      Isolation is her accustomed state.

      She has no idea how to proceed.

      She feels lost.

In spite of the temptation to succumb to depression and give up,

      she continues sincerely in her determination

      to seek admittance to the royal realm.

      Because of her sincerity

      something happens that seems entirely unremarkable

      but will affect the wanderer forever after.

      A fellow comes along who is of the realm of light.

      He does not look fancy;

      he looks ordinary, plain, even simple.

The wanderer considers,

      Even though he looks like just a commoner,

      I will ask him for directions to the king's court.

      She expects little from the plain-looking person,

      yet experiences something special about him.

      She is too distracted, though, to heed her experience—

      she just wants the information

about entering this special place,

that is all she can think about.

The wanderer asks the fellow,

Would you please give me some advice?

I have been trying to enter this land of the king,

but I cannot.

To her surprise, the plain-looking person responds simply,

Are you qualified?

Am I qualified?

I need to be qualified to enter the world of joy and clarity?

I thought I could just go in.

The plain person says to her,

Well, yes, you can.

You can just enter.

The wanderer asks,

Why don't I, then?

Plain person,

Because something appears to be stopping you.

The wanderer thought she had already accomplished her goal

but now sees there is quite a way to go;

she has only scratched the surface.

Feeling a deep yearning to be an insider,

the wanderer sincerely asks the plain-looking person for help.

Impressed by her sincerity,

       the simple person from the inside helps her

       to come through the entrance into the king's realm.

       Then he tells the wanderer,

       There are four gates within the royal realm,

       and to attain to the very center, the king's court,

       the place of your desires,

       you have to go through all four of them.

Seeing that she is eager to do what she must to advance,

       the plain-looking fellow takes her to the first gate.

       She reads the inscription carved into the stone above the gate,

       proclaiming the initial phase of the royal realm...

KNOWLEDGE

Clear away all illusion of separateness and imagined interference
        as you travel with the wanderer.
        Continue to be sincerely focused,
        deeply relaxed
        and fully present.
        Be receptive to this experience.

The person tells the wanderer,
        If you want to be in the royal realm,
        the realm of great privilege and enjoyment,
        the realm of illumination and fulfillment,
        you have to have knowledge.

The fundamental knowledge is,
        you belong in the royal realm.
        You belong here because you are part of it.
        You must also know
        that you do not belong in any place of which you are not a part.
        Remember this.

The wanderer hears these words—

> 'You belong in the royal realm because you are part of it...
> you do not belong in any place of which you are not a part'—
> and the words are simple,
> but he understands them not.

He looks around and he sees splendor.

> Life here feels fresh to him,
> like spring, with flowers and birdsong and burbling brooks.
> The sounds are the music of nature,
> the joyous expressions of pure vitality.
> The landscapes are open and clear,
> brilliant in their display.
> He feels suffused with a gentle, luxurious comfort
> and confidence.

But he wonders,

> How can I belong here?

He asks the plain-looking person,

> What do you mean I am part of this realm?
> I am from somewhere entirely different.
> I am from a place of darkness and dirt, murk and slime.
> How can I be part of this magnificent realm?
> I am not!

Here is where a guide is of utmost importance.

> The wanderer is stuck in confusion caused by attachments
> to false ways of thinking about himself

that he formed in the world of murk.
Due to his mistaken conceptions
he does not know himself in reality.
He regards himself the same
as the dismal world whence he came.
He considers himself as arid and empty, bleak and worthless,
and of the same fabric as the desolate place
in which he dwelled for so long.

The kind person points out to the wanderer,
If the queen has invited you into her realm,
it is because she knows you belong here.
You could not come into this realm unless you were of it!
You must understand you are part of this realm
and part of its people.

He continues,
You must know what it means to be in this realm,
and what it means to not be in this realm.

Why does he point this out? wonders the wanderer.
Everything this person does and says has meaning.
'To be in this realm' and
'to not be in this realm'
are not the same.
I must not be superficial or careless about his teachings.

The plain fellow says,
Likewise, you must learn to differentiate

between the ways of being that bring you to the royal court

and those that lead you away from it.

This knowledge you must possess.

That seems fundamental:

what brings me to my goal

and what leads me away from it—

that I can learn.

The fellow from the realm says,

Learn to know from your own experience,

not from hearsay,

not from belief.

Allow your experience to direct you

toward the real knowledge within.

Learn to know from your own Experience,

not from Hearsay,

not from Belief.

Allow your Experience to direct you

toward the real Knowledge within.

Learn to proceed from clear and unbiased observation.

When you have experienced something in clarity,

you can say, 'I know this to be so.'

To accept something just by belief is lazy

and potentially detrimental:

you could too easily be misled.

Therefore I say to you,

Don't ever believe me;

experience for yourself the truth of what I say.

Be observant in all your moments.

Learn from your learning experiences.

Learn from your learning Experiences.

That is the Way to gain real Knowledge

and pierce the Membranes of Falsity and Habit.

Living in real Knowledge means Living true to yourself.

The wanderer is struck by the significance of this fellow's words.

He says to himself,

I have had many experiences throughout my life,

yet have not really learned until now.

I have meandered from experience to experience,

and only now have I found my way

to the realm of my yearning.

It dawns upon the wanderer

that every time he consciously pays attention

and absorbs what this helpful person says to him,

it propels him directly toward recognition of his path
and of himself.

Even though the queen welcomed him,
he did not know how to enter the royal realm.
A few thoughtful words from this fellow
have given him meaningful direction toward his goal.
The wanderer recognizes within himself
the growth of a deep respect for this person from the inside:
He has more wisdom than I expected!

The wanderer says,
Pray tell, you have guided me to this point,
perhaps you could help with something else:
how do I know I will learn what I need
to succeed on the path through the four gates
into the core of the king's realm?

How do I know I will overcome
the temptations, distractions and distortions that are so habitual
and that constantly, even now, attempt to pull me back
into the familiarity of the gray and lifeless land?
How do I know?

My desire is clear,
but those old negative patterns are strong.
I often do not discern between
that which brings me to the king's court
and that which pulls me back toward the land of confusion.

The wise person points out to him
> that he has raised an observant question.

The wanderer continues,
> I fear becoming lost.
> I remember how easily I was distracted from my path
> even after meeting the king.
> My patterns of distraction and distortion are so strong that,
> although I am sincere, I fear losing my way again.
> And I fear losing my life
> before I am able to complete my journey
> to the heart of the queen's realm.
> What can I do?

The person from the realm answers,
> You have to find a guide.

The wanderer feels lost again,
> How do I recognize a guide?

The person states calmly:

> A true Guide is a Person whose Words and Way of being
> help you experience Reality:
> he speaks straightforward to your Core
> in Words that reverberate within you
> and awaken the Knowledge that resides there.
> *Thus* you recognize your Guide.
>
> A real Guide will lead you to the Core of the King's Domain
> for he has traveled the Path
> and knows how to help you find your Way.

The wanderer asks,

> How do I find such a guide
> who will open my eyes and my heart
> so I can experience the clarity and fullness that *you* experience?

And it dawns upon the wanderer

> that she is asking for guidance about finding a guide
> from someone who has given her nothing but guidance.
> She asks the person of the realm
> about this strange phenomenon.

The plain person smiles

> and tells the wanderer to ask herself
> if she can possibly see what is transpiring.

Faced with this responsibility, the wanderer simply states,

    I am asking someone who has been guiding me

    for guidance in finding a guide.

    I wonder what is behind this,

    why a part of me refuses to see the guide?

The simple person asks her,

    Why do you think it is?

The wanderer ponders this sincerely and says,

    I fear if you were to be my guide,

    I would have to give up the world whence I came,

    for you would guide me to dwell in the king's realm,

    the realm of joy and ultimate satisfaction.

    I would have to think of myself

    as someone of this royal realm

    and give up thinking of myself

    as someone belonging to the realm of murk.

The fellow responds,

    Yes...?

The wanderer deliberates out loud,

    I want to go to the core of the realm of light and fulfillment,

    but something within me still refuses

    to give up the painful murky domain.

The person says,

    Why don't I help you then

    return to the world whence you came,

the world of pain and sorrow?
There you can collect all you left behind and bring it here
through the four gates
into the royal court.
Then you can have both:
you can have pain and suffering
and be in the realm of joy and contentment.

No, says the wanderer, that makes no sense.
I do not want that!
Why did I struggle so hard to come to the luminous realm?
I want to leave behind forever the land of pain and sorrow.
I want to stop wallowing in the gutter
with slime, rodents and fleas.
I do not want to infest the realm of purity
with all that depravity.

Then she hears what she just said,
and she understands:
this caring person has guided her
through her own inner experience
to resolve her dilemma.

The wanderer realizes that the irrational fear
of not being able to return to the familiar world of suffering
is a false seduction
inflicted by the negative habits and attachments
that run so deep.
She decides,

in spite of old patterns wanting to interfere with her fulfillment,
she is making a choice.
The wanderer makes the choice
now and forever to be in the royal realm.

She feels clear,
she feels strong.
She realizes it is not even a matter of choice;
certainly the world of pain and sorrow
is not an option she wants.

Is the world of pain and sorrow an option for you?

Nor is it an option to bring the familiar misery into the royal realm
and pollute it.
She wants only the realm of clarity and joy
and knows that the person of the realm
can guide her to its core.
She does not want to give her patterns any more opportunities
to return her to the world of darkness and confusion.

She determines to secure herself
from the temptation to ever return there,
for she knows those delusive urgings are not hers,
they are the urgings of the mute patterns of the past.
She no longer identifies with those patterns;
she will no longer give them loyalty
or any other form of her energy.

The wanderer further realizes she has been reluctant

to acknowledge the person of the luminous realm as her guide

because *he sees her as she is*!

He sees her as she is,

and he accepts her unconditionally.

She understands

that she has not yet learned to accept herself unconditionally.

Even worse, she has a life-long history of not really relating to herself.

Her initial reaction to the open way he addresses her was fear.

Now however, from the conduct

with which this friendly person relates to her—

with unwavering respect, attentiveness and trust—

the wanderer is beginning to see herself

in a more favorable light,

with self-respect and appreciation.

She now wants to relate to herself fully and deeply, with trust.

The guide talks to her about trust.

It is a difficult issue

because the wanderer has had her trust violated,

as have most of us,

from early childhood on.

She was so afraid to trust

that she walled herself in with the most destructive mistrust—

mistrust of herself.

She knows that if she wants to expand in her experience

to the security that is inherent to being in touch with herself,
she has to completely break down those walls of mistrust.

> Mistrust of yourself
> is the Wall that isolates you most from all.

The wanderer realizes,

> When there were moments of meaningful,
> close being-together with the guide,
> I recoiled by not heeding his teachings
> and finding things wrong with him.

Why is her relationship to the guide so tenuous and challenging;

> why does she at times relate to him
> as if he were some strange creature?
> The wanderer realizes that the guide constantly relates to her
> in the directness, honesty and closeness
> that indicate his perception of her
> as one who is far beyond the little, separate thing
> she is used to perceiving.

The guide explains to her,

> The perception of yourself
> as a limited and isolated *body-mind construct*
> is fundamentally and totally false.

This false self-identification is called *ego*
and is the root-cause of human suffering.

The Perception of yourself
as a limited and isolated body-mind Construct
is fundamentally and totally false.
This false Self-identification is called Ego
and is the Root-cause of human Suffering.

In the realm of murk, the guide is a threat to the ego.

Ego protests, 'You are making me do things:

you are making me stop suffering,

you are keeping me from being isolated,

you are trying to force meaning and intimacy into my life,

you are trying to force reality upon me.

I am too busy and not ready—

not today, not this week, not this lifetime.

This is a threat to me.'

The guide gazes gently upon her,

Your real identity is characterized by interconnectedness.

Can you realize interconnectedness all by yourself?

If you *reject* intimate relationship,

warm and close and trusting,

with someone who gives you the most important experiences

of your life,

who treats you with love and care,

honoring the fullness and glory of Being that you are,

with *whom* will you have relationship?

And if you will not have a relationship with such a *one*,

how can you have a relationship with the *all*?

The sages since ancient time have taught

that you cannot have a relationship with all-pervasive *Being*—

the essential power by which everything *is*—

without having a relationship with a guide.

To be practical and real in your quest for fulfillment,

you must find a guide and establish the relationship firmly,

clearly and fully.

Often people wander aimlessly through life

before they find a real guide.

They ask, 'How do I find a guide, how do I recognize one?'

It is said, 'When the student is ready the guide will appear.'

However, you need to create your own readiness,

so when you find a real guide,

you allow yourself to recognize him

and delve into the relationship fully and unhesitatingly.

When you recognize that you have found a real guide,

to benefit, you need to relate to him with trust.

You will soon find that lack of trust in yourself

is your main obstacle to trusting the guide.

I fear I cannot sustain a trusting relationship with the guide,
    nor with myself, says the wanderer.

The guide replies,
    That is why you suffer from *depression*.
    You fear to sustain the clear experience of yourself;
    therefore you give up on yourself,
    you deaden yourself to self-experience.
    The disregard of self-experience
    is the fundamental cause of depression.
    You settle for the accustomed experience of emptiness.
    Nothingness.
    Thus you feel you need not fear disappointment—
    things cannot get worse than the life of nothingness.
    Here you have an expression of distrust of yourself:
    you do not trust in your ability
    to conduct your life successfully—
    a self-fulfilling prophecy of utter failure and hopelessness.
    Without choosing to trust yourself,
    you will also not trust the guide.

> The Disregard of Self-experience
> is the fundamental Cause of Depression.

Who says you cannot sustain a relationship

with what you know to be real?

Since you know you need to have oxygen in your blood,

you just keep breathing, you do not question it.

You can apply the same matter-of-factness

to keeping your faculties in contact with who you really are.

If you *had to* create a system by which to stay alive,

would you create one?

Certainly you would.

Just as certainly you are able to create a system

that ensures your faculties remain

in clear relationship with yourself.

Be practical, become well educated and *expert*

in knowing *how to live true to yourself,*

and then really live that way.

Thereby you override all your opposing tendencies.

How can I tell whether a guide speaks truth or illusion?

That is a very important question, says the fellow.

When you sincerely involve your instruments of perception—

your body and mind, your senses, feelings and emotions,

your intellect and intuition—

a real guide's teachings reverberate in your heart.

You will know the truth of those teachings

through your own clear experience.

When this takes place, you know you have found your guide.

Someone who recites from books may be a guide of sorts
>but is different from one who speaks from *direct experience.*
>A guide who speaks from his own direct experience
>reveals reality by guiding you through experiences
>that lead the sincere student to the realization of true identity.

When you have even just one such experience,
>you can be sure you have met a true guide.
>If, on the other hand, you have many such experiences
>and still do not recognize the guide,
>you are keeping your faculties behind a wall.

The guide tells the wanderer of his own experience:
>I met my guide in the sacred mountains
>and knew immediately that he was a true guide;
>I had no question about it.
>I also knew of my readiness to commit myself
>to a relationship in which I hide nothing,
>where I am real and related to as real.

The guide is eternal Being
>whom I love, adore and cherish.

The first requisite of a true relationship with a guide
>is to find yourself worthy—
>worthy of being in a relationship
>free of hiding and pretense—
>and to be ready for unconditional acceptance.
>This is difficult for people in the land of murk.

They treat themselves as if they were only worthy
to be orphans or outcasts.

The wanderer knows he has a tendency to distrust,
but he knows even more strongly
that he wants the full experience of self-trust.
In relationship with the guide
he can safely break down all the walls of suspicion.
As he more deeply entrusts himself
to the relationship with his guide,
he learns to trust himself and the whole of reality.

The guide finds it necessary to repeatedly prove to the wanderer
she is worthy of trust.
She has difficulty knowing her own worthiness
because she does not yet completely trust herself.
The guide relates to her in terms of the power he sees in her,
not the suspicion and disempowerment
with which she relates to herself much of the time.

She is clear now;
she wants to experience herself only as who she really is,
and she wants to present in relationships
only her genuine Being.
She does not want to present a front anymore
and will no longer weave webs of deception,
rationalization and distortion,
for they cover her real beauty and glory.
She determines to be a person of integrity:

to consciously be who she is
and not live in pretense and falsity.

He determines to be in a relationship of wholehearted honesty
in which he is accepted and related to—
including by himself—
as he really is.
He will be in true relationship.

He *wills* to trust himself.
No longer will he maintain all the skillful ways
he has developed over the years
of camouflaging distrust of himself.
He makes a conscious determination to live in self-trust.

Have you made the conscious determination to live in self-trust?

Thus, with sincerity and firm resolve
he turns to the plain-looking person and asks,
How can I persuade you to be my guide?

The person answers,
You approach the guide properly.

The wanderer takes this in.
She reflects,
'You approach the guide properly.'
He did not say how.
I know from my experience with him
that he always has a reason for what he says or does not say.

The wanderer is learning to trust her knowledge
derived from *experience* with this gentle Being.
She focuses within herself again
and experiences deeply what she just learned.

The wanderer feels the light coming on.
She realizes,
As I trust this person to be my guide,
I trust myself in relation to what he teaches me.
I trust myself!

She turns to him with determination and with great joy.
In integrity, with trust, sincerity and deep commitment
she appeals to the person from the luminous realm
to grant her the great boon
of accepting her in a lasting relationship
as her guide on the path to her final fulfillment
in the core of the royal realm.

The guide tests her sincerity and her readiness:
What is your highest priority?

To live true to who I really am.

This is good.
Living as someone who you are not
has you missing out on your *real* life.
Thus living according to your true identity
is of fundamental importance
and is the *ultimate practicality.*

To live true to who you really are,

>you need to know what your true identity is.
>
>This I will help you experience
>
>when you are established in the relationship of absolute trust
>
>with your guide.

I am determined to live permanently and irrevocably

>in that relationship
>
>with you, my guide.
>
>Therefore:

I vow with my full Integrity to live true to my real Identity.
I shall live true to who I really am
now and forever,
continuously and without Backsliding.
From this Moment on I will do all Actions
in Fulfillment of this Vow.
It is so.

The guide accepts her into this most powerful, honest

>and interconnected relationship.
>
>This is her initiation.
>
>Her *initiation.*
>
>It is her initiation into relationship with the ultimate reality.
>
>She discovers it to be the relationship with herself.

Now she feels so much better prepared
to travel on the path to the core of the king's realm.

The initiation is simple and profound.
The aspirant recognizes her initiation
as an utterly important gift
that can ensure her success on the path
to the realization of her highest potential.
She firmly determines within herself
to always relate to this gift with integrity:
to be unfailingly true to herself,
to her guide
and to this empowering covenant.

The relationship with her guide is pivotal to the initiate
on her quest for the core of the royal realm
and fills her with delight beyond her dreams.
She is inspired with great energy and hope.
Her life is full of promise, light and opportunity.

Joyfully her eyes open now
and she sees what she could not see before,
as if layer upon layer of veils just dropped away
leaving her with brilliant vision.
She sees herself and accepts herself
in the experience of direct, real knowledge,
the experience of *Inner Knower.*
In this state
she allows the effortless flow of her thoughts and feelings,

unhindered by likes and dislikes,

or altered by judgment.

Thus she becomes free to experience what *is*.

The aspirant discovers something that makes her heart leap:

she trusts this inner knowing unconditionally.

Thus it is clear to her now

that she trusts her guide unconditionally,

for the guide speaks to her

in the language of the Inner Knower.

In the trust of herself and her guide

the aspirant feels a strength and safety

deeper even than what people are said to experience

when they are dreaming of being in the womb.

Through her profound experience she feels so empowered,

so utterly secure in herself,

that she feels she can do anything.

She is certain she will live in the royal realm.

Now, with a vigor and enthusiasm

unlike anything she has ever experienced,

she is ready to proceed on her path.

She cares not how long it will take,

nor how many gates she will have to go through,

for she feels connected and filled with calm confidence.

He looks forward to traveling the path through every gate

and feels freed from fear and hesitation.

Freed from fear and hesitation.

A vibrant sense of ease suffuses him

because he has unburdened himself from doubt

and enmeshing attachments

to the world of confusion and suffering.

He feels safe and trusts himself.

With their relationship now established,

the guide leads the initiate through experiences

that help him cease the meaningless meandering

in his thoughts, feelings and emotions,

and in all his actions.

He will no longer drift passively through life

in distraction and confusion.

He will proceed directly

toward his fulfillment in the royal realm.

Our aspirant sees that his steps are now in accord with his true desire

and are leading him toward the fulfillment

of his innermost yearnings.

He grows strong and comfortable,

familiar with, and trusting in, his knowledge.

This allows him to expand the horizons of his consciousness

beyond the limits that seemed absolute

when he lived in the land of hopelessness.

With the expansion of consciousness,

she is able to absorb all the lessons

and proceed through the realm of knowledge
with even greater ease and familiarity.

Through her guide,
> whom she now sees as a beloved, luminous Being,
> she learns that knowledge is true experience
> of anything and everything in the royal realm of reality.

The guide helps her to realize a most important lesson:

All that deserves to be called Knowledge is of Reality.
Knowledge is not to be merely accumulated
or just thought about.
Knowledge is to be lived.
This is the genuine Way to respond to Reality.

She begins to understand
> the interrelationship of everything in the realm.
> She is not sure how it comes about—
> mysteriously, everything is interconnected.
> Knowledge of one aspect connects the knower
> to knowledge of other aspects of the royal realm.
> Her mind does not have to coordinate all the little details,
> for she no longer relates to knowledge
> as a mere collection of facts.

> Everything is interconnected.
> Knowing one Facet of Reality gives Intimations of other Facets.
> One Facet reveals the others—
> as well as the Whole of Reality.

Having found the secret of knowledge
> and being firmly committed to the realm of knowledge,
> the aspirant grows toward wisdom.

She cannot tell how long
> her progress through the realm of knowledge has taken.
> And she cares not.
> She knows now that she is able to dwell in knowledge;
> the realm of knowledge is hers to live in.
> She has gained access to the limitless knowledge
> that resides within her.
> She has knowledge of freedom from the world of futility,
> pain and suffering.
> She has knowledge of how to live in success,
> joy and dynamic enterprise.
> Before, she identified with weakness;
> now she has the knowledge to be in full power.

She experiences a wonderful sense of integration,
> being at one with herself in beautiful knowingness.

She is powerfully invigorated and inspired

by the wealth of knowledge she has discovered.

Her heart overflows with joyous gratitude to her beloved guide.

Thus our aspirant, filled with confidence,

arrives buoyantly at the second gate.

In wondrous joy she reads the inscription...

GATE TWO

THE SCIENCE OF SELF

Prepare yourself now so you may, in your own experience,
be joined with our aspirant
as she is about to enter the next level.
Sincerely cause your mind,
as well as your other faculties,
to be continuously attentive to yourself
in your center, the area of your heart.
Like the aspirant, be suffused with trust in yourself.
Be in joy.

The guide says to the initiate,
In passing through the first gate,
you attained fundamental knowledge of your Being
and openness to truth.
This empowered you
to advance toward the center of the royal realm
and to approach this, the second gate.

I want to comfort you with this thought:
although you have had but a brief exposition of knowledge,
this knowledge is integral to and indicative of

the *entirety* of knowledge.
Now that you have united with a real guide
who relates you to the royal realm,
and you have grasped the fundamental bead of knowledge—
that you belong to the royal realm—
you can grasp the entire strand:
the science of Self.

> Once you unite with a real Guide
> who relates you to the royal Realm,
> and you grasp the fundamental Bead of Knowledge—
> that you belong to the royal Realm—
> you can grasp the entire Strand:
> the Science of Self.

I use the word 'science,' says the guide,
> as indicated by its root, *scire*, to know.
> Real knowledge, as you have learned,
> comes from direct experience of reality,
> of that which fundamentally and irrevocably *is*,
> irrespective of opinions, circumstances and conditions.

Real Knowledge comes from direct Experience of Reality,
of that which fundamentally and irrevocably *is*,
irrespective of Opinions, Circumstances and Conditions.

The initiate says to his guide,

What do I need to do to master the science of Self?

I am eager to dwell in this realm.

Whereupon the guide lovingly advises him,

The first requirement is for you to continuously remember

you belong here in the royal realm.

You belong here;

you learned this in the realm of knowledge.

Now you must experience

that not only your body and mind belong here,

your very *essence* belongs here.

Yes, says the initiate,

and then he halts.

What is my 'essence'?

After a brief silence, the guide replies,

It is what you *essentially are*.

Your essence is the underlying, irreducible substance of you,

the very power by which you *are*.

It is that without which you could not be.

Your essence is the real you.

That is what we name *Self.*

Your Essence is the underlying, irreducible Substance of you,

the very Power by which you *are.*

It is that without which you could not be.

Your Essence is the real you.

That is what we name Self.

Remember always, says the guide,

Self is your true identity.

Self is who you *really* are

substantially, not superficially,

permanently, not momentarily.

Self is your true Identity.

Self is who you *really* are

substantially, not superficially,

permanently, not momentarily.

The guide asks the initiate,

Do you know who you *essentially* are?

In your mind, as what do you identify yourself?

Do you think of yourself as a man, woman or child?

A brunette, blonde or redhead?

Plumber, doctor, householder?

You are none of those.

> You are not the superficial, changing Things.
> Neither Gender nor Job nor Looks define you.
> Nor are you Feelings or Emotions.
> You are that which you have always been,
> that without which you could not be.
> You are what you are in Essence.
> Impress this deeply upon your Mind
> and never forget.

What is it without which you could not be?

You could not be without the power to *be*,

the *power of Being.*

Your *Beingness* is the undeniable, unchanging,

definitive essence of you.

The guide knows the heart of the initiate

and knows that she hears

but does not yet understand these fundamental teachings.

However, knowing his student's sincerity,

he trusts in her willingness to bear *not* comprehending
while she applies sufficient determination and alertness
to bring herself to understanding.

Think about this, the guide continues:

There is an energy, a power, which causes you to be
and causes everything about you to be.
Regard your body, for example.
Your body is composed of cells—you know that.
The cells that compose your body are made up of atoms.
Atoms are defined as the smallest portions
into which an element can be divided
and still retain its properties.
Atoms are made up of a dense, positively charged nucleus
surrounded by a system of electrons.
You could regard an atom—
a great sage of this royal realm once said to me—
as 'energy momentarily concretized.'
The space between the atoms that compose your body
is far greater than the atoms themselves.
Let that sink in for a moment.

You, dear reader, allow this to sink in.

Furthermore, these atoms constantly come and go,
while you, in essence, remain the same.
Although the cells that composed your body in your infancy
are gone,
you are still the same essential one

who was born on the day of your birth.

So you see, in reality

your body is not a solid or permanent object,

but an energy system in constant flux.

How about your mind?

Your mind is not an organ,

it is not an object.

What is it then?

Your mind is just energy,

a particular kind of energy

by which you are able to experience *that you are.*

And so it is for all your faculties,

for your feelings and emotions,

your intellect and intuition,

even your body and senses,

for every facet of you:

particular energy systems by which you can experience

that you are!

Thus, fundamentally,

everything about you is the energy by which you *are*

and by which you *experience* that you are.

That same energy empowers you to *express* that you are,

that you are being.

Not only are you *being*,

but you *are* Being.

The power by which you are is the irreducible essence of you.

It is *who* you are.

Being is your identity.

The power to be is who you really are.

Not only are you *being,*

but you *are* Being.

The Power by which you are is the irreducible Essence of you.

It is *who* you are.

Being is your Identity.

The Power to be is who you *really* are.

Could a time or place *be* where there is no *being*?

No, it is self-evident, that could not be.

Does Being begin or end?

Can you imagine a time when Being was not or will not be?

No, of course not.

Being is all-pervasive, unbeginning and eternally unending.

The Power of Being is

all-pervasive,

unbeginning

and eternally unending.

The guide gazes intently into the eyes of the initiate
to ensure she gives her full attention, and says:

> Everything that is,
> is because of the Power to be.
> The Power to be is the Essence,
> the Identity of everything.
> Everything essentially is the Power of Being.
> All is Being.
> You are Being—the Power to be.

I know you are not accustomed to thinking of yourself this way
because of your false conditioning in the land of murk.
However, the fact is, your identity is what you are in essence.

> Your Identity is what you are in Essence.

The guide says with calm force,
In essence you are Being;
that is the reality of you,
the reality of everything:
the reality.

Since Being is unbeginning and unending,
you are eternal transcendent Being.
Transcendent because Being *is*,
independent of—therefore beyond—time and space,
circumstance and condition.
This is the real you.
This is Self.

> In Essence you are Being;
> that is the Reality of you,
> the Reality of everything:
> *the* Reality.
> Since Being is unbeginning and unending,
> you are eternal transcendent Being.
> *Transcendent* because Being *is*,
> independent of—therefore beyond—Time and Space,
> Circumstance and Condition.
> This is the real you.
> This is Self.

The guide makes sure he has his initiate's full attention:
For you to know this is of fundamental importance—
to know not just the words,
but to know through your own experience.
Thus, tell me now

from your experience of what I have taught you,
What is your true identity?

The aspirant has been deeply present
in the experience of what the guide has shared with her.
She answers with the clarity and certainty of experience,
I am the power by which I am,
the power without which I would not be:
the power of Being, Self.

*Do you consistently think of yourself
in terms of your essential identity?*

Excellent, says the guide. And he asks,
How are you true to that?

She answers without hesitation,
By *living* as the power of Being that I am.

How do you live as the power of Being? the guide asks.

Again she replies with certainty,
By thinking, feeling, acting
as the self-knowing Being that I am.

The guide asks,
When do you live like that?

She answers immediately and with conviction,
Now and forever, continuously.

The guide asks,

>   What if circumstances and conditions change?

She states now with an inner strength,

>   The reality of Being never changes,
>
>   it is permanent and invariable.
>
>   Therefore I will live true to the Being I am
>
>   irrespective of circumstances and conditions.

The guide challenges,

>   What if some time you feel differently
>
>   and would like to consider other options?

She responds directly,

>   There are no options other than reality.

Are you *clear about that?*

The guide continues warmly, Excellent.

>   What will also help you
>
>   is to learn *how* the people of the royal realm live true to Self.

First understand this fundamental fact:

>   the king is the source of all,
>
>   the king *is* all,
>
>   and—at the same time—the king is *beyond* all.
>
>   It must be clear to you now
>
>   that the king is the power of Being,
>
>   the essence and identity of all.

Being is the Source of all,

Being *is* all,

and—at the same Time—Being is *beyond* all.

The Power of Being is the Essence and Identity of all,

the Unity of all.

The guide continues,

> Therein lies the subtle interconnecting link
> that unites all forms of Being.
> Not only is all knowledge interconnected,
> as you have already learned,
> all Being is interconnected.

You need never feel alone again,

for you have many Brothers and Sisters

on the Path to Fulfillment in the limitless Realm of Self.

From his relationship with the guide

> and from his own experiences,
> the initiate is now able to savor
> his essential interconnectedness.

Savor your essential interconnectedness.

He feels empowered, calm and confident:

> his self-trust has grown,
>
> and he is secure in his ability to maintain this trust
>
> in full integrity.

He knows that every time he relates to who he really is,

> he experiences utter trust.
>
> Thinking, feeling or intuiting about himself with trust,
>
> he has certainty and tranquility,
>
> peacefulness and power.
>
> He is filled with deep loyalty to the Being that he is.
>
> This allows him to experience even greater moments of clarity
>
> —indeed, of illumination.

How do you relate to who you really are?

The initiate is illumined from his very core,

> an illumination that emanates from and bathes the Being he is.
>
> He delights in these beautiful experiences.
>
> He feels empowered and inspired.

No longer a stranger,

> a lonely wanderer drifting aimlessly through life,
>
> he feels included now.
>
> He travels with a strong sense of direction
>
> and no longer feels like a foreign visitor
>
> in the bountiful realm of the king.

So the guide continues,

> The interesting thing about this realm is,

the king is everyone who dwells here.

Anyone you see in this realm is the king

who welcomed you at the great portal in the beginning.

Furthermore, the queen has immediate knowledge of everything.

Everything is available to her,

everything is connected to her—without limit.

Limitless Being and limitless knowledge are one.

All the apparent diversity that you are accustomed to seeing

is an amusing play the queen set into motion

for her own entertainment.

She makes herself appear in many guises,

yet always is the same queen, the same king.

This you must learn to know and understand

through your own experience.

If you want to live in the realm of fulfillment,

you live here as a member of the queen's family.

You live here as the queen lives,

for the queen is everyone.

The aspirant asks,

How does the queen live?

The guide says with calm emphasis,

Royal Being constantly lives

in the fundamental awareness of the unity of all.

It is of cardinal importance

that you do not relate to your knowledge of interconnectedness as a mere intellectual notion.

Remember always that interconnectedness is the reality of all.

That *includes* you.

In the land of ego, continues the guide,

> if someone were to tell you about interconnectedness,
>
> you would exclude yourself in false modesty:
>
> 'All is interconnected except for little me.'
>
> Do you see how egotistical that is?

> To see yourself separate and isolated from the Cosmos
>
> in which all is interconnected,
>
> is the Height of egotistical Thinking
>
> and displays Ego's Folly.

How do you see yourself?

Thus, says the guide,

> to live as royal Being lives,
>
> you constantly think and feel and act
>
> in the fundamental awareness of the unity of all.
>
> Therein lies your fulfillment.

> To live as the Power of Being lives,
> you constantly think and feel and act
> in the fundamental Awareness of the Unity of all.
> Therein lies your Fulfillment.

The king lives in bliss.

> When you live as the king lives,
> you live in bliss.
> Bliss is inherent to the experience of Being.
> In the royal realm
> you live free of the distortions regarding your identity
> that kept you bound to the world of suffering.
> It is the purpose and meaning of your life
> to live in the bliss of Being that you are,
> to live in joy,
> to live congruent with real Self.
> That is *Self-realization.*

It is the Purpose and Meaning of your Life
to live in the Bliss of Being that you are,
to live in Joy,
to live congruent with real Self.
That is Self-realization.

The guide, aware the aspirant is in the experience of his teaching,
continues,
This is how royal Being lives.
You realize you *are* all
thus *have* all.
You *have* and you *are* power and truth,
self-love, trust and joy,
strength, peace and serenity.
Remember that, live that, be that.
Each of these royal qualities is a direct connection
to your experience of royal Being.

Have this be your experience of these teachings.

When you identify yourself as royal Being, says the guide,
you think, feel and act entirely opposite from someone
who identifies himself
as a person from the isolating, painful, murky land.
You are all-pervasive, unbeginning and unending Being.
Thinking of yourself as eternal Being—

one who never ceases to be—
affects the way you feel.
That feeling, in turn, profoundly affects your actions.
Remember, your thoughts affect your feelings,
your feelings motivate your actions,
your actions, in turn, affect your thinking.
The cycle is complete.

You are all-pervasive, unbeginning and unending Being.
Thinking of yourself as eternal Being affects the Way you feel.
Thoughts affect your Feelings,
Feelings motivate your Actions,
Actions, in turn, affect your Thinking.

Imagine, while *knowing* that you are the all-pervasive power of Being,
you continued in the tendency to *think* of yourself
as limited, sinful and unworthy.
This would be self-contradictory.
Such contradiction would keep you
from being congruent with yourself.
Everything about you would be tied up in deep conflict.
Do you understand now
why so many in the land of murk live in conflict?
Once freed of the self-contradiction
inherent to thinking of yourself negatively,

you are free of inner conflict

and therefore at ease and released from restrictions.

In the realm of bliss,

the way you move, the way you behave,

is profoundly different

from the way you were in the murky world.

In the royal realm you do not walk around

with your face sadly dragging on the ground.

You are not anxious, fearful or depressed.

You live as royal Being lives,

joyful and content.

If you do not live as royal Being,

your behaviors oppose who you really are.

Thus your behaviors confuse and frustrate you.

They invariably result in dysfunction, failure.

If you are angry and sad,

attached to distrust, isolation and self-disregard,

you are incongruous with your essence;

you are in a state of imbalance and self-opposition.

That is a principal cause of illness.

In harmony with Self, you experience health—

physical, mental, emotional and spiritual health.

You can choose to cause everything about you to live as royal Being.

The guide gazes lovingly upon the aspirant and speaks to her gently:

Now there are still times when you *need*.

When you attune yourself to royal Being—
to who you really are—
you need not.

Now you still *want*.

When you know yourself as a member of the royal realm,
you want not.

You know what it is to feel like an outsider—apart, isolated,
as if you were merely a visitor.
Now that you know yourself as a member of the royal realm,
you never feel apart or on the outside,
you never feel isolated.

The initiate listens with sincerity and deep focus.

She treasures each point of knowledge the guide presents to her
and absorbs herself in all she learns.

The initiate says,

I understand what you say to be true, but my habits persist.
I ask you sincerely, my guide, what do I do to free myself
from the patterns established during my murky past?
Those patterns of thinking, feeling and acting
tend to enslave me.
I fear those patterns.
Please help me know what to do.

The guide, convinced of the aspirant's sincerity and readiness,
initiates her into yet deeper secrets
of the realm called the Science of Self.

First, the guide teaches his beloved student restraint.

Restraint.

He speaks to her with the strength of clarity:

If you want to live in this realm, you live like the queen.

You cease behaving like a guttersnipe,

like a citizen of the land of suffering.

To overcome the patterns that bind you to suffering and pain,

you must purposefully practice behaviors

that contradict the patterns of your past.

You are in charge of your life and your behaviors;

the patterns are not, no matter how persistent they may seem.

Thus you *restrain* your body—every fiber, every atom—

and your senses and feelings,

as well as your mind, intellect and intuition

from their habitual involvement

with the old, negative behaviors.

You will immediately experience

your power over those patterns.

To overcome the Patterns that bind you to Suffering and Pain,
purposefully practice Behaviors that contradict them.
Restrain your Body, Senses and Feelings,
your Mind, Intellect and Intuition
from their habitual Involvement
with the old, negative Behaviors.

Remember always that the negative behaviors have their origin
in the false perception of you as isolated, fragmented—
and therefore flawed—ego.

When you notice you have kept your body in a state of tension,
for example,
purposefully induce release and relaxation
through every organ and system and even cell of your body
by the subtle application of your will.
See to it that you maintain that healthy state
throughout your life,
no matter what the circumstances and conditions.
You can.

You restrain your mind and all your other faculties
from ever again relating to you
in terms of a false perception of who you are.
Restrain your feelings from enmeshment with *depression*—
a much cultivated state in the land of murk—
as depression denies your ability to experience yourself
in the joy of Being.

You simply accomplish this restraint
by attuning yourself to the awareness of who you really are:
empowered Being.

Anxiety and fear are symptoms of ego.
You wipe them out permanently

by sincerely relating to yourself as conscious Being
that you are.

Restrain yourself from ever again engaging in *ego-actions,*
     such as dishonesty, greed and pride,
     attitudes and actions based upon
     your previous perception of yourself
     as an isolated and limited entity.

You restrain yourself by—again—
     calling forth the experience of yourself
     as someone far beyond
     the limited person to which you have been conditioned.
     About this you will find out much more as we continue.
     When you know your real identity,
     you know that those old behaviors are not congruent with you;
     they are false and are the cause of suffering.

Do you restrain your faculties from the negative behaviors of ego?

Take careful note of this, says the guide:
     by *restraint* I do not mean *repression* or *denial.*
     You accomplish overcoming negative behaviors and actions
     most effectively by a powerful positive approach:
     you achieve great success and self-empowerment,
     not by wrestling with negative patterns,
     but by sincerely enacting positive behaviors.
     Do this positive practice with continuity,
     with expertise and trust in the Being that you are,

and you will free your faculties
from enmeshment with negativity.
You will transform
your instruments of experience and expression.

> You achieve great Success and Self-empowerment,
> not by wrestling with negative Patterns,
> but by sincerely enacting positive Behaviors.
> Do this positive Practice with Continuity,
> with Expertise and Trust in the Being that you are,
> and you will free your Faculties
> from Enmeshment with Negativity.
> You will transform
> your Instruments of Experience and Expression.

The guide points out,

> This is your mission:
> to transform the functioning—even the character—
> of your faculties.

The aspirant says,

> I am sincere and determined.
> I trust in your guidance.
> I trust in myself.

Please reveal more to me
so that I will be expert at living the Self I am.

The guide is moved by the aspirant's wholeheartedness
and helps her to experience even higher levels
of the science of Self.
He explains,
The king is vitally aware, from moment to moment,
of the limitless extent of his Being.
He is aware of all the manifestations
through which he *projects* himself and *experiences* himself
in his *unitive state*: self-knowing oneness,
Being experienced in clarity, spontaneously,
from moment to moment without end.
Allow this to take hold in you.

Be open to experiencing and expressing yourself
on these expansive levels.

In the realm of reality, says the guide,
you live according to an ethical, moral way
predicated upon your understanding
of your intimate interconnectedness with all creations.
The queen *expresses* herself in the awareness
of interconnectedness with her creations;
she also *experiences* herself through such self-expression.

The queen knows that all her manifestations—
all creatures large and small—are self-expressions,

and she harms them not.

To live as the queen lives, you cultivate *harmlessness*.

In the land of darkness,

> where you wandered the murky grounds
> and fell into the pit of despair,
> you considered everything and everyone as competition,
> even as a possible enemy.
> Now that you know the fundamental truth
> and recognize everyone as being one with the king,
> relate to everyone and everything with harmlessness.
> Never harm anything.
> You do not want to harm your awareness of Self
> who is expressed through all.

The guide speaks emphatically,

> Knowing the queen is all
> and knowing your *interconnectedness* with the queen,
> you need not want.

> You cannot want more than the Infinite.
> There is no more.
> You need not be avaricious when you have all.
> Let go of Greed and Want.
> There is no Need for you to amass more of your limitless Self;
> the Attempt is absurd.
> Greed and Want are rooted in Ignorance of your Identity.

He continues,

> There is no need for you to compete with other manifestations,
> for all manifestations, in essence, are Self.
> You need not compete with yourself.

There is no need to lie, cheat or steal;

> restrain yourself from perpetrating those behaviors
> unto yourself.
> Do you think there is ever an advantage to lying to yourself,
> to cheating yourself, to stealing from yourself?
> You will only think so
> when you suffer from the mistaken idea of yourself
> as significantly less than you are.

In this, the royal realm of reality,

> you learn to live in accord with your essence,
> your spirit, your true identity, Self.
> You live in harmony with all manifestations of royal Being.

You live *sincerely, consistently, expertly, with trust in yourself*
in constant recognition
of the interconnected Being that you are.

To be successful and fulfilled,
live sincerely, consistently, expertly, with Trust in yourself
in constant Recognition of the interconnected Being
that you are.

Through the science of Self
your faculties become astutely observant,
and you learn to promote within yourself
those ways of being
that are true to a member of the royal realm.
You become *self-observant*.

What do you mean by that? asks the aspirant.

The guide answers with clear emphasis,
Focus your observing powers—your faculties—
upon the Self you are.
This is the real reason for your faculties to exist:
to relate to the Being that you are.

> The principal Reason for your Faculties—
> your observing Powers—to exist,
> is to relate to the Being that you are.
> Therefore focus your Faculties
> upon Self.

Cause every one of your faculties to live with great attentiveness
>   to the all-inclusive Self;
>   cause your faculties to work for you.

Remain focused;
>   *you are worthy of such attentiveness.*

As their relationship has grown closer, the guide shares from his life:
>   When I was a young student
>   I practiced painting with watercolors weekly
>   at the royal Art Museum.
>   I spent hours painting watercolor renderings
>   of a royal chamber.
>   Having had no experience with watercolors,
>   I had difficulty with them.
>   Yet they required of me to act as spontaneously as I could.

One time, while I was deeply absorbed in this demanding task,
>   my attention was suddenly drawn to something else.
>   I had not heard anything,

nor had I seen anything

other than the painting I was absorbed in.

Yet something beyond my task attracted my attention.

I looked up and saw a small group of people

on the other side of the great chamber.

I immediately sensed

that one of them was not an ordinary person.

The group drew nearer to watch me paint.

They introduced this person to me

as the future king of their land.

He was not wearing special robes,

nor had his presence been announced by fanfare.

The pure presence of royalty, in a calm and unassuming way,

exerted a magnetic attraction upon all around him.

They attended to him with complete devotion.

I tell you this story, says the guide to the aspirant,

to illustrate how *you* should be related to.

As you have learned,

you are in the royal realm because you belong here.

You belong here because you are *of* this realm.

You are royalty.

The royal Being that you are

deserves to be treated with attentiveness and care,

with devotion and honor,

even more than that future king.

Is that how your mind relates to you? he asks her.

> Do your feelings and emotions, all your faculties,
>
> constantly attend to you
>
> as the royal Being that in essence, and in fact, you are?
>
> If not, they are not fulfilling their purpose.
>
> They are not serving *you*.

The guide continues,

> In the science of Self you learn to cause your faculties
>
> to attend to and relate to the Being that you are—
>
> not to objects, circumstances, conditions
>
> nor any other momentary phenomena,
>
> not to false ideas,
>
> not to emptiness,
>
> not to distractions,
>
> but to the royal Being that you are.

Here, you live in constant recognition of your royalty,

> of the Beingness that you are:
>
> you think and feel this way about yourself;
>
> all your behaviors relate to you and express *that you are*;
>
> every part of you, every faculty
>
> lives in acknowledgment of the Being that you are.
>
> Thus you learn to accept yourself unconditionally.
>
> This is the foundation of loving yourself.
>
> Being loves being.

Being loves being.

You are nurtured in this realm so deeply
      that you celebrate and savor
      the moment-to-moment experience
      of eternal Being that you are.
      You learn to love and cherish
      the power and beauty of royal Being,
      the Self of all, the source of all.
      As the essence of all that is,
      Self is the essence of all experience.
      Remember, all experience essentially is *of* Self *by* Self.
      The *experiencer* and the *experience* as well as the *experienced*
      are one: the conscious power of Being, Self.
      Self is the experience and the joy and pleasure of all.

> The Experiencer and the Experience as well as the Experienced
>
> are one:
>
> the conscious Power of Being,
>
> Self.
>
> Being and the Experience of being
>
> and the Joy of being
>
> are one.

The guide addresses the aspirant with a deep sense of joy:

When you appreciate Self more than all else,

when you are devoted to Being,

everything about you—all your faculties—

are attracted to the reality of Self

and are thereby transformed.

Is there in you such a great devotion to the Self of all

that your faculties are powerfully attracted

to the reality of Being?

Is there in you *such a powerful devotion to the reality of Self?*

If your faculties hanker after illusion or distraction,

continues the guide,

if something else takes priority over Being,

then your faculties, led by your mind, will not serve you.

Your faculties will be enmeshed in falsity.

Your faculties' enmeshment in falsity
>is the cause of your life in the gray, murky land.
>Everything about that place denies the reality of you;
>therefore it is antithetical to you.
>Life in the world of falsity is diametrically opposed to you
>and has you living in irreconcilable conflict.
>This results in confusion, self-opposition
>and the accompanying doubt, frustration and depression
>with which you were so familiar in the murky land.

Life in the World of Falsity
is diametrically opposed to Self
and has you living in irreconcilable Conflict.

The aspirant experiences a strong sense of calm
>as the guide continues:
>In the king's realm you are free of the desire
>to distort or change your experience of reality.
>You are also free of the desire
>to distort the experience of your identity;
>you are free of the need to hide behind delusion, self-deception
>and deception of others.
>You recognize the Self that you are in all power and beauty
>as you experience and express yourself

in unconditional self-acceptance,

for you recognize Self's perfection.

Do you relate to yourself with unconditional self-acceptance?

The guide makes the simple statement:

> The Self you are is perfect.

The difficulty is that you have identified yourself

as someone you are not,

which in its very nature is imperfect

because that *someone-you-are-not* does not exist.

That is why you have always considered it preposterous

to think of yourself as perfect.

In the murky world,

your behaviors did not express the Being that you are.

Your behaviors expressed a mistaken idea of you,

thus they expressed someone unreal, non-existent,

therefore imperfect.

In the murky world

your thinking, feeling and acting expressed imperfection,

and thus you identified yourself as *im*perfect.

In the royal realm you recognize that you are Being.

Everything is Being.

Being is the all-pervasive reality.

Being is limitless.

This is the truth of you and the *all* of you.

Being is the truth of all, therefore perfection.

In the science of Self you are devoted to truth.

When you live in the royal realm,

you never feel the need to distort truth.

You love truth, for the Being that you are *is* truth,

and you have learned to love Self.

Never distort what is so infinitely beautiful.

The Power that causes all to be is absolutely beautiful;

it cannot be improved upon.

When you experience the limitless beauty,

the divine and underlying harmony in this realm,

there radiates from within your core

a constant sense of contentment.

Here you are at peace with yourself

and with what is.

You are one with the eternal and all-pervasive power of Being

that is the essence of all that is.

Thus you *have* everything.

There is no cause to ever be discontent.

Realizing that Being is the source of all that is
frees you from all need
and therefore from discontent.

> Realizing that Being is the Source of all that is
> frees you from all Need
> and therefore from Discontent.

When you live in discontent, you deny the reality of Being,
you deny the wholeness of what you *are*,
thus, of all you *have*.

In the denial of the Being that you are,
you try to amass what cannot be amassed.
Your need for having more objects
or certain people
or particular circumstances and conditions
is but a distortion of your *innate* and *real* need
to experience yourself in infinite interconnectedness with all.
You cannot amass infinity.

Remember, you cannot overcome the Sense of Isolation
or be content,
by amassing the Objects of the World to yourself.
Nor will you ever be at Peace
while you try to change Circumstances or Conditions
by naming them other than what they are.

To be truly fulfilled,

all you need to do is acknowledge who you really are
and—most importantly—*live* that!
Live true to the Being that you know you are.
Uncover the contentment inherent to essential Being,
let it unfold,
and you will experience your interrelatedness with all,
the intimate interconnectedness with the king.
The king is Being in fulfillment.

The aspirant listens with attentiveness and devotion.

In the presence of her guide
she experiences deep understanding.
The guide hears the initiate express great wonder,
joy and excitement
coming from the depth of her own experience.
Yet, the guide knows her understanding is still limited,
and so he takes the aspirant further.

Experience this, the guide says to the initiate:

> as a citizen of the queen's realm you accept yourself,
> you acknowledge yourself,
> you even praise yourself, the Being that you are.
> No longer do you oppose this
> with the false protestations of ego.

And light dawns again within the initiate:

> he understood what his guide taught him about contentment,
> but he knows now that he was not ready for contentment,
> for his experience was held back
> by an underlying assumption of his unworthiness:
> Contentment is not for me because I am unworthy.
> He had adopted this assumption of unworthiness
> in the land of murk
> and carried it with him throughout his travels
> like some secret talisman.

Do you relate to yourself as unworthy or as ultimately worthy?

The guide lovingly says to him,

> You are a member of the royal family
> who is worthy to be in the queen's court.

The aspirant is flooded by a deep sense of relief.

> He feels a release that purifies him:
> release from having to be ready for flight,
> release from defending and pretending,

slinking about and hiding.
He feels free.

Now he is able to present himself to his guide
with even deeper openness and simplicity,
with clarity, free of false assumptions,
with honesty.

And there are many more lessons for him in the science of Self.
The guide reveals:
In the royal realm you recognize your body
as the physical vehicle of your soul, your essence,
and you respect it as such.

This vehicle consists of the *vibratory modes* of the material realm
and is subject to them.
With the same respect you have for the universal king,
here you regard your body, your vehicle, as his chariot.
You fine-tune it, clean and polish it.
You make it move smoothly, easily.
You learn to hold your body in high esteem,
in effortless balance.
It is with the awareness of your essence
that you most powerfully affect the vibratory modes
that compose your body:
you relate to your body in congruency with who you really are
and thereby create harmony
throughout your physiological systems,
resulting in health and strength and fluent effectiveness.

Gracefully poised, your body no longer hinders your endeavors

nor distracts you *from* them or *with* them.

Thus your body is a fit vehicle for the Being that you are.

You also realize

that the queen has generously distributed her energies

to animate all objects, including your body.

She animates all your faculties,

including your communication systems,

such as your nerves and senses.

Thus, sincerely endeavor to align all that is alive in you—

your body, senses and mind,

your emotions and feelings,

as well as your intellect and intuition—

with her *animating energy.*

Through the careful control of your breath,

which carries the animating energy,

you learn to establish a controlled relationship

with her all-pervasive energy,

a relationship of harmony and confluence.

In the murky world,

you developed the habit of compulsive involvement

with things that do not give you satisfaction:

your mind constantly chased after them

and received only frustration.

You cannot live in the realm of totality

and chase after fragments as if they were the whole;

that is living in contradiction to reality.

The inevitable result is suffering in conflict.

Therefore you learn to withdraw your mind

from its habitual involvement with fragmentation

and unite it with the light of knowledge within you.

Thus your mind is able to perform its intended function:

to serve you in the conscious experience

of the fundamental fact that you are.

When your mind fulfills its original function,

you find enormous strength and great power within yourself.

This is akin to the power one man found

when he faced—without sufficient weapons—

a great enemy fleet.

He took a magnifying glass and turned it to face the sun.

With the glass he concentrated the sun's rays

and directed them at the enemy sails.

Using just that small piece of glass,

he burned down the entire enemy fleet.

Such is your power

when you withdraw your mind from dissipating involvements

and concentrate it upon a *chosen point*.

You burn out all attachments, distractions and hindrances.

> Withdraw your Mind from dissipating Involvements
> and concentrate it upon a *chosen Point*
> to burn out all Attachments, Distractions and Hindrances.

In the king's realm,

> you learn to concentrate your mind
> and all your energy patterns—all your faculties—
> into one powerful wholeness.
> You are then able to apply them to the point of your choice
> and burn away the dross that stands in your way—
> the dross of forgetfulness,
> of hesitancy,
> of mental murkiness
> and dissipation of energy.

Through the practice of concentration

> you hone your instrument, the mind, into a powerful force
> and overcome patterns of distraction and procrastination.
> With those negative patterns
> you remove your mind from true intention.
> With concentration you learn to focus on the essential.

For much of your life, my friend,

> you have dissipated your energy
> by keeping busy with the meaningless,

thereby depriving yourself of experiencing the essential.
Focusing your mind will prevent that.

The aspirant is aware how much of her life she has given away
> to wallowing in the murk of the meaningless.
> Again she finds herself impressed
> by the depth of the guide's teaching.

Have you given much of your life to the pursuit of the meaningless?

She reflects on how her relationship with her guide—
> and therefore the relationship with herself—has evolved.
> In the beginning she saw the guide only as a simple laborer.
> After learning to know him,
> she was able to perceive the beautiful essence of this person.
> She experienced how consistently the guide cared for her:
> he always related to her with unmitigated respect
> while presenting to her the most luminous wisdom.
> Due to having been treated in this manner,
> she overcame her fears
> and her habitual patterns of isolation.
> She overcame her attachment
> to feeling limited and self-doubting
> and found the courage to petition him to be her guide.

The initiate works hard at the lessons from the guide.
> Nevertheless, it does occur sometimes—
> especially when she forgets to be focused—
> that fear creeps in again.

During such times,

she resorts to fear as if fear were her refuge.

Fear her refuge!

Fear keeps her in the familiarity

of her experiences in the land of murk;

no change is required of her.

If she were to go deep into the realm of contentment,

she would lose her citizenship in the land of suffering.

She forgets her learning experiences:

there is no advantage whatsoever

to living in the land of suffering,

no benefit, nothing positive!

Fear has her regard the dark world as her home,

even though when she dwelled there

she was painfully aware it was not her home.

Faced with the irrational fear

of not being able to return to the land of suffering,

she needs to learn not to be seduced by the negative habits,

no matter how deeply they are impressed.

During times of weakness and confusion,

the aspirant's thoughts—in spite of all she has learned—

still fall into the irrational tendency to doubt herself:

Maybe I did not make the right choice.

This guide does not have a long, flowing, white beard,

he does not touch me with a magical feather,

he does not wear saffron robes,

and he displays no miraculous powers—
maybe I chose the wrong guide.
That's why I'm having all these problems,
these resistances and confusions.
It must be all his fault.

Now however, her initiation vow to always be true to her guide,
to always be true to who she really is,
comes to her aid.
She resorts to her integrity and she recognizes,
This thinking is a distraction;
it arises from old patterns
that are trying once more to assert themselves.
I have already felt in my heart
the deep connection with the guide,
and I have experienced great trust.
I have already petitioned him to be my guide.
Awake!
Arise from this stupor.
I will remember what I have learned
and I will live in accord with it.

Then the struggle is gone,
and looking back she wonders why it even arose.
She has just gained a higher level.

The guide teaches her:

> Forgetfulness of your Identity is the Cause of your Problems.
> You open the Door to forgetting your real Identity
> when you neglect nurturing your Self-experience.

Negligence regarding self-awareness allows forgetfulness to creep in.
    Forgetfulness breeds ignorance.
    With ignorance, pride comes to the forefront.
    Pride will interfere with your path through the four gates,
    the path to fulfillment.
    When you find that forgetfulness or ignorance or pride
    has led you astray,
    you need to admit to yourself
    that you have invested your energies in a blind alley.
    Do not doom yourself like someone
    who takes the wrong path and refuses to turn back
    because he will not admit he made a mistake.
    Pride is costly.
    Pride is a symptom of the ignorance inherent to ego.

Pride is a distorted Opinion of one's Worth.
This inordinate Opinion is an Attempt to compensate
for Feelings of Insecurity regarding oneself.
The Root-cause of such wayward Thinking is Ego—
the false Conception of oneself as isolated from the Whole.
Ego is based on Ignorance and Illusion.

The guide continues,

When you are in the awareness of the real Self,

the power of Being you really are,

you are free of pride.

Remembering your true identity always frees you

from the temptation of traveling on paths that dead-end.

Living according to your true identity

saves you from suffering.

When your mind is in balance and reason,

you know this to be so.

Remember, your mind's function

is to reflect the knowledge that you *are*.

Mind's fundamental Purpose is to reflect Awareness of being
to the Being that you are.

While you may rejoice in clarity

    and savor the interconnectedness of Being,

    your ego can spoil that brilliant experience by asserting,

    'I will bring about this experience all by myself.

    You cannot trust anyone but me because I am the expert.'

    Yes, ego is the expert of binding you

    to the murky world of despair.

The initiate recalls the experience of recognition deep in his heart

    when the guide's teachings first moved him.

    He is honest enough to be receptive

    to the memory of this recognition

    and to acknowledge to himself, again,

    that the guide has always shared profound wisdom with him.

    This wisdom is part of him now,

    because the guide has helped him to actually *experience* it.

    He has experienced knowledge so directly

    that he *knows* it to be true.

He remembers that precious moment

    when he overcame his ego pride and isolation

    and petitioned the plain-looking person to be his guide.

    He knew the attachment to his painful past was too strong,

    too complicated,

    for him to advance alone, all by his ego-self.

The aspirant sees clearly,

    Ego will never help me into the king's realm.

    She has come this far through the help of her guide.

And she remembers the common observation:
when you arrive somewhere you want to be,
stay with the vehicle that brought you there.
She is aware of the dangers to which she almost fell prey.

Through her relationship with the guide,
> she constantly learns to appreciate
> her own strengths and capabilities.
> Again, she wonders
> why she sometimes made it so difficult for herself,
> why she has, at times, been so afraid to be open
> to the love and guidance so generously given to her.

She remembers how she once feared the guide.

There are times when caution, or even skepticism, is good.
> In the murky land,
> people are attracted in great numbers
> to guides who promise to bestow fulfillment upon them—
> 'I'll do it all for you'—
> but give only falsity
> and thus disappointment.

False guides violate the truth by wielding deception.
> When the aspirant identified herself with the world of murk,
> the falsifiers seemed attractive
> because they are *of* the murky world.
> They were attractive to those aspects of her
> that wanted to stay in the gray realm;

they offered familiarity and its false comfort.
But she knows now that this guarantees only suffering.

The false ones offer the rewards of murk
    and disguise it as that which your heart seeks—
    the teachings of the realm of fulfillment.
    The false guides attract people
    who are enslaved by feelings of lack and need.
    They promise *they* will overcome your resistance
    without you having to do any traveling
    through the four gates in the queen's realm.
    These promises appeal to the ego,
    to the sense of separateness and need.
    False guides play upon weaknesses:
    low self-regard and consequent fear, anxiety and depression.
    They play upon the patterns by which people are bound.

The initiate feels a sense of gratitude toward herself
    for having saved herself from the pain and suffering
    of such distraction.
    Her travels on the path have already yielded to her
    so many joyous experiences
    of adventure and discovery and beauty.
    She forges the unitive bond with her guide even more deeply
    and feels joyously renewed
    in her progress toward the royal court.

She acknowledges to herself,
    In this simple man, who has become such a friend to me,

I constantly experience brilliant clarity.

Through the clarity and beauty I experience in the guide

I am also aware of the clarity and beauty in myself.

This is a discovery of profound importance.

With renewed sincerity,

she endeavors to live the knowledge of Self,

to think of herself as self-knowing power of Being,

to breathe that, to sense that

and to acknowledge

that the color and brilliance of the royal realm are *in her*.

Do you live in such clarity and beauty?

The guide gazes lovingly upon the initiate and says,

Up to this time, we have been building the foundation

and making preparations

for your awakening to total integration

with the realm of fulfillment.

Now comes an important step

to entering the deeper levels of the realm,

to which you have been looking forward.

I will teach you the fundamental requirement

for *inhabiting* the royal realm:

the secret of meditation.

> Meditation is being in the Joy of limitless Consciousness
> from Moment to Moment,
> free of the Misconceptions of Separateness, Limitation and Need,
> as well as all the accompanying Suffering.

And the guide asks the initiate,

> Would you like me to guide you
>
> through an experience of meditation,
>
> the experience of being in the clarity of Self,
>
> the experience of being Being,
>
> continuously and free of distortion,
>
> by applying the skills you have learned
>
> of remaining focused with trust in yourself?

Oh yes, says the initiate, I am ready for that.

You are invited to participate with the initiate in this experience.

They sit together on the grass of a beautiful meadow

> suffused with clear morning light.
>
> The sounds and scents of nature embrace them.
>
> They are at peace.

Let yourself be at peace now.

The guide says,

> Sit up straight

in effortless balance
with your body relaxed.

Follow along sincerely, step by step.
Do not just read this, do *it.*

Cause your breath to flow in natural rhythm.
Withdraw your mind from all outward going tendencies
and bring it inward
by devoting its full attention to simply observing the breath.
Henceforth you will keep your mind focused
on a point of your choice.
For now, as your breath enters through your nostrils
and exits again,
have your mind observe without comment,
just observe.
Breath enters your body through your nostrils,
goes to your lungs
and smoothly flows out again.
Soon you notice that your mind quite naturally comes to rest
in the area where your breath goes,
which is also the area of your heart.
Invite your mind to be steadily present and at home here.

Determine you will sincerely continue
to devote your mind to this experience.
Allow yourself to be present in a wonderful, relaxed focus.
My voice now is your inner voice in self-acknowledgement.

Consciously cause your whole body to relax deeply.

> You can bring that about
> by focusing the powers of your mind
> upon any part of your body you choose
> and telling that part, 'Relax now, let go.'
> Even if you have not done this before
> you will find that you have great ability
> to deeply affect your body's state.

You can start with your feet.

> Send your feet the signal to relax
> and they *do* relax.
> Feel relaxation streaming through your feet and then upward
> through the ankles,
> into your calves—relax your calves, *feel* them relaxing.
> Send relaxation flowing into your knees,
> all around and throughout your knees,
> and into your thighs—cause your thighs to relax—
> all the way up to your hips and pelvis relax, relax.
> From your feet up to your back
> let relaxation flow freely,
> relax, relax, relax.

Now send relaxation flowing up your back,

> from your lumbar area
> to your ribcage,
> into your shoulders.
> Feel your entire back

suffused by the healing energy of relaxation.

Especially feel your spinal column

permeated by this releasing flow.

Vertebra by vertebra relax,

including the soft tissue in between,

as well as all the nerve strands traversing the spinal column,

relax, relax, relax.

Send relaxation throughout your entire back

and feel the letting go, the opening up.

Relax your back, relax.

From your shoulders,

send the relaxation down through your arms

into your hands

through the tips of your fingers,

let go, let go.

Hands and arms and shoulders be relaxed.

Now cause relaxation to flow from your shoulders into your neck

and feel release throughout your neck.

Every little muscle and bone of your neck, relax.

From your neck,

send relaxation streaming into your head.

Tell your head to relax.

Feel the relaxing wave of energy flow

from the top of your head

down through your forehead and temples and brow.

Relax, let go, relax.

Steadily go along with this now; this is your *experience.*

Let go even in your eyes,

> and your nose, relax.
>
> Feel your mouth go slack,
>
> along with your tongue and jaw.
>
> All the little facial muscles become smooth and relaxed.
>
> Your entire head relax, inside and out.

Do you feel it?

Cause the relaxing flow of energy to radiate through your throat

> and into your chest, relax.
>
> Let your chest feel open and expansive, free.
>
> Relax your abdomen,
>
> a place where you may store much tension.
>
> Release, relax your abdomen, relax.
>
> And into your loins relax, let go, relax.

Now to the insides of your body—

> even if you do not know
>
> the exact location of your various organs,
>
> send them the signal to relax and they *will* respond.

Start with the kidneys in the small of the back

> and tell them to relax.
>
> From there, cause the whole reproductive system to relax.
>
> Then send the healing energy up through the anus, colon,
>
> intestines and stomach, relax.
>
> Even if you do not feel the specific parts,

simply send the signal and they will respond, trust in that.

With repetition trust will turn into proof;

you will be astonished how profound the effects are.

Relax your liver on your right side,

just below the bottom edge of the ribcage.

And relax your pancreas and spleen near the stomach, relax.

Relax your lungs,

have them feel open and free

as your breath flows evenly and easily.

Now your heart.

Your heart serves you steadily even while you sleep.

Please invite your heart to relax.

Relax deeply, heart, release, relax.

Flow more evenly and easily and just a bit more slowly.

Relax dear heart, relax.

And your brain.

Tell your brain to relax.

Just have it go into a state

in which it suspends all unnecessary activity.

Let it rest.

Have your whole body relax now, inside and out,

including every organ and all your systems

down to the cellular—even the molecular—level.

Feel it all in one unimpeded flow of total relaxation.

Throughout this deep-reaching process of autosuggestion,
    cause your breath to flow in natural rhythm—
    this is really important.
    Be aware of breath
    as the carrier of the *animating* form of energy
    that empowers every aspect of all life.
    Consciously cause your breath to flow in harmony with nature.
    Observe the effortless flow of your breath.
    Simply observe—like an impartial bystander.
    Do not comment, just observe.
    You are the *Silent Observer.*

As before, follow your breath as it enters through the nostrils
    and proceeds to your lungs
    and flows out again, making room for the following inhalation.
    Be aware of the fluid continuity
    between inhalation and exhalation.

Relax,
    just observe
    as the natural rhythm of your breath
    helps you go deeper and deeper
    into conscious experience of yourself.
    You are simply being.

As you inhale now and follow your breath to your lungs,
    you experience a sense of expansiveness.
    Feel the expansiveness.
    There is no need for you to *cause* that to happen,

simply allow yourself to *experience* the expansiveness
as it spontaneously occurs.
Similarly, as the exhalation occurs,
experience the beautiful sense of letting go
and being in the purity that naturally accompanies
the outgoing flow of your breath.

You too, let go, relax,
remember to remain focused in this entire experience.

Continuing in the experience of yourself in expansiveness and release,
you become aware of the area that the breath goes to,
the general area of your heart.
The luminous sages refer to it as the *cave of the heart.*
Regard this as your *center.*
With the inflow of breath
you feel the area of your heart expanding with awareness,
an inner luminosity—
again, *allow* this to occur—
and with the exhalation
you experience a beautiful sense of release and purity
in the cave of your heart.
Just rest here, be at peace.
You are not *doing* but *allowing* the experience.

With your focus conveyed by your breath
to the area of your heart,
you become increasingly aware of this area.
Feel your energies converging here, in your center,

especially your mind,

a principal element in leading all your faculties

through this experience.

Invite your mind to consider the area of your heart as its home.

Tell your mind,

'I want you to rest here, make yourself at home, relax.

You need not perform any functions now.

Just be present here, relaxed and balanced.

Be still, be calm, be at ease.'

Feel your mind luxuriating in the comfort and safety of its home,

the cave of the heart, your center.

Center.

Your feelings naturally are drawn here too,

along with your intellect, intuition and senses;

they flow along with mind, their coordinator.

Visualize your faculties seated in your center,

effortlessly balanced.

They are comfortably at home in the cave of your heart,

in harmony within themselves and with each other

and with you,

in unity.

You may choose to be in the same peaceful, balanced,

centered state.

Have your faculties devote their continuous attention to you,

the *indweller* of the center

who is aware of Self now.

You experience yourself as Self, your *real* identity:

the power that is your essence and the essence of all that *is*,

the power of Being that you are.

You are Self experiencing Self as the all-pervasive one Self:

Self in self-awareness,

aware of being aware,

consciousness without limit.

Be wholly absorbed in that.

Silently witness your mind

as it shines with the knowledge of who you are

and rests in tranquility.

Your feelings are at ease,

your emotions at peace.

Everything about you is balanced in your core,

in harmony, deeply relaxed.

Your breath expresses the rhythm of eternal Being

as it relates awareness to the center.

See yourself dwelling in the very bosom of the royal realm.

As you continue in this state,

your mind is ever more attracted to this beautiful experience

of being at home,

deeply relaxed and at peace,

absorbed in consciousness, the awareness of Being.

This makes it easier for your mind to resist

the false allure of distractions—

mind's meandering in thoughts unrelated to the task at hand—

that tend to enmesh mind in matters

that cause you to suffer in dysfunction, deprivation

and disappointment.

Growing immune to such dissipation of focus,

your mind grows into a persistent state of empowerment

in faithful devotion to consciousness

and therefore to being in continuous unity with real you,

the self-experiencing Self that you are.

Dwell in that.

Consciously dwelling here

in the infinite abundance of the king's realm,

you never want anything else.

Thus you dwell here in continuity and totality.

You dwell here on your own volition

with unhindered enjoyment.

Remain in this realm from moment to moment,

breath to breath,

experience to experience,

and joyously engage in the experience of yourself

in the limitless realm of Being.

This is the state called meditation.

Meditation.

Continue in this state of self-experience

as you go on with your life.

Abide in self-awareness and be at peace in the joy of Being.

Now, says the guide,

> stretch out your arms overhead,
> inhale and exhale deeply.
> Look around and see the multifarious ways
> by which the queen expresses herself.

Oh, says the initiate,

> never before in my life have I had such beautiful experience.
> I feel sated with joy, I am fulfilled.
> How can I remain in this state?

Excellent question, says the guide.

> The most effective way to stay
> in this beautifully balanced state of consciousness
> is to remain sincerely and continuously focused
> in the awareness of your true identity:
> the power of Being, the interconnected Self
> who belongs to the universal royal realm.

The guide continues,

> Thus you live in the state of meditation without interruption.
> This is the royal state in which you live loyally,
> once and for all.
> Every moment is to be experienced
> in the awareness of being the Being you are,
> not just when sitting like this,
> but during all your activities.

You let go of the conception of yourself
>   as someone from the world of murk;
>   you let go of that world as your heritage and your habit;
>   you let go of the misconception
>   that the land of darkness is your home.

You *know* and consciously *assert*
>   that you belong in the realm of light,
>   therefore you continuously, and only,
>   *live* as the self-knowing royal Being.
>   You will learn more about enacting your life true to Self
>   once you pass through the next gate.

Thus, living in the realm of joy—of limitless Being—
>   is not to be related to as a mere practice;
>   it is your inherent way of being,
>   the way that has to be permanent to be real.

The guide continues,
>   This lesson will not take hold in you
>   if you allow yourself to live foolishly,
>   if you let unreality sway you to believe that you are not worthy,
>   that you are not of the all-encompassing royal realm.

You will not realize the limitless joy
>   of eternal self-knowing blissful Being
>   as long as you think there is something else more desirable,
>   even your unworthiness.

You cannot be in the Experience of Being
if you are attached to non-being.
To be in the Fulfillment of the Realm of Self
requires your unconditional Commitment
without Hesitation and without Reservation.
Nothing is more desirable.

Thus you make an absolute determination within yourself—
with unwavering integrity and loyalty to the Self you are—
to live henceforth true to your real identity, true to reality.
Now—and again, for this is of cardinal importance—
you not only make the *determination*,
but you institute the *action step* that ensures
you will henceforth only live true to this determination!

The guide cautions our aspirant,
This will transform all your inspirations and determinations
into reality.
Assess carefully whether you are ready to take this step.

The aspirant finds this challenging to think about.
Again the fear of losing her place in the dark land asserts itself.
That fear would have her hope for *dual citizenship*,
but the law is, you can claim only one.

> You can be loyal to only one,
>
> be it Reality or
>
> be it Falsity.
>
> Every Moment, with every Behavior and Action,
>
> with every Way of being,
>
> you make the Choice:
>
> to be true to Reality, to Self,
>
> or to be in Falsity, in Ego.
>
> Not making a Choice is making a Choice:
>
> it is the Ego-choice by Default.

She thinks about this again,

> I know that I do not belong to the world of suffering,
>
> but even now my mind and feelings are affected by it.
>
> The murky atmosphere still seems familiar;
>
> I lived there so long.

The initiate draws upon her learning experiences:

> I know the realm of real Being is what I want with all my heart.
>
> Even if I could not have all the joys of which you speak,
>
> I would still want to be in the king's realm
>
> because it is true,
>
> it is real.

I hear my mind's little nagging voice lying to me:

> 'I don't know if I can stay in this beautiful realm;

do I have what it takes?

Can I trust myself to see it through?' And on and on...

However, the moment I remember

the suffering in the gray land,

I immediately feel how horrible it is there.

Experience yourself now as the aspirant in self-assessment.

Why should I choose the murk of ignorance and illusion

over the clarity of knowing Self?

Why should I choose pain and suffering in falsity

over the joy of being in truth?

Why should I choose the horror of being *unconscious,*

as if comatose,

over the bliss of being vibrant and alive in *consciousness?*

Why fear, why doubt?

Nonsense!

Do you feel that?

Our aspirant faces herself with honesty born out of true self-interest:

The patterns and habits within me

still attempt to lead me toward suffering in ignorance,

but I will not allow those tendencies to mislead me.

I have spent my life struggling against the painful place

where I knew I did not belong.

There I suffered nothing but misery, illness,

anxiety and fear.

Those impulses are not of my Being,

but of non-being.

Who is in charge here?

My life does not belong to old patterns and compulsions.

As of now, I put my foot down,

I do not permit them to act as my masters.

This is *my* life.

I claim control.

I am committed to the realm of reality, the realm of fulfillment.

I know who in reality I am.

I make the choices here and I choose to be true to myself.

This I choose, consciously and in full integrity!

In the depth of my core the knowledge of Self is clear,

and I focus on this in continuity, in meditation.

This experience inspires my thoughts and feelings,

even my intuition—everything about me.

This is what I choose to live by.

Thus, every time I receive the impulses

that try to tear me away from my experience of Being,

I will assert the knowledge of my real identity—Self—again.

And it is important for me to remember,

every time I suffer in the negative states,

it is due to my having forgotten

to remain in the Self experience.

The guide hears that the initiate acknowledges her inspiration.

Inspiration is her response to the urgings of the essence,

the spirit that she is.

She is relating to herself

as an aspirant on the path to fulfillment

in the *realization* of Self.

And the aspirant continues,

I understand clearly now how meditation—

the continuous experience of who I really am—

is the focal point and the culmination

in this realm called Science of Self.

Experience along with the aspirant as she says within herself:

I claim the experience of Being that I am.

I choose to proceed toward Self-realization.

This is the decisive step by which I will grow in empowerment

as I proceed steadfastly toward the core of the royal realm.

This is not just another promise I make.

As of this moment I act and function and live

true to the self-knowing Being that I am—

irrevocably and continuously!

This is the final and never-ending action I now take.

I have completed another struggle,

the struggle I caused

by not going directly into the queen's loving arms,

the struggle of attachment

to the apparently binding power of the gray world.

I have loosened myself from that attachment decisively

and burned the bridge:
>I am leaving no possibility open to return there.

I feel light, I *am* light.
>I am free.

My commitment to being in the experience
>of the power of Being that I am
>is absolute.
>I live in the integrity and fullness of that commitment.
>I seek no refuge in the world of confusion.
>My refuge, my joy is the realm of reality.

In this moment of deep clarity
>the aspirant feels again a release washing through her.

Feel this!

The problems that seemed so complicated and overwhelming
>are simply washed away by his *enactment* of the commitment
>to live in truth the Being that he is.
>All he feared he now sees clearly
>as figments of his imagination, as illusion!
>The obstacles he saw everywhere in the land of despondency
>are only of that place,
>and he has no need or desire
>to recreate them in his imagination ever again!
>He leaves behind the world of fear and anxiety.

He says to his guide,

> I am done with hesitancy and attachment,
> with that which only hurts, clouds and confuses.
> I reaffirm my commitment.
> I am on my path to the core of the royal court
> to take my place amidst the king's family.

Now true to himself,

> he is able to fully experience
> the state of unconditional self-acceptance.
> This opens to him the potential of love.
> He sees why this realm, filled with love,
> is so brilliant and lively with color.
> He now understands the state of love.
> He discovers his ability to live in love,
> to think and feel and breathe love with every fiber of his Being.
> He is able to experience love with every faculty,
> savoring the fullness and clarity of Being.

With great satisfaction, with joy and transcending pleasure,

> he dwells in the realm of Self, free of distortion.
> He dwells in meditation,
> in a deep-seated and secure sense of abiding bliss,
> and experiences himself—knows himself—in luminous clarity.

The aspirant is suffused by elation.

> He feels secure, for he realizes he has learned to be expert
> at breaking through all obstacles
> and advancing to the core of the royal realm.

He enjoys the wonderful connection with his guide
and is ready to proceed.

The guide, with a joyful twinkle in his eye, says,
Now you may look forward to the next step:
the third gate is before us.

The aspirant walks toward the third gate
and gazes with wonderment at the inscription...

GATE THREE

THE MEDITATION OF ACTION

With the power realized by traversing the realms of knowledge
and the science of Self,
you, the aspirant, proceed with great energy and enthusiasm
and with eager anticipation to the next phase,
utterly free of fear.
Be present to yourself
and be present to the guide.
Savor your experience
as you open yourself to entering a realm
where you will gain deep insight.

The guide invites the aspirant,

Enter this profound realm.

Here you will find beautiful experiences and powerful lessons.

In the realm of murk, says the guide,

you continually created your own suffering.

When you entered the royal realm,

you began to learn how to permanently cease suffering.

You learned you are *of* the royal realm,

and you learned what it is like to dwell here.

On your journey to this point
you have undergone much preparation, development
and learning.
Now you enter the third realm
where you directly reap your rewards
by learning to *express* the Being that you are,
not just while you are in those specially chosen moments
seated in a comfortable position,
but in all moments of your life,
in all circumstances and conditions
and through all your actions.
That is the continuous experience of *action in meditation*.
To realize the meditation of action,
you need to have a firm foundation of meditation.

In Meditation you dwell
in the State of continuous Consciousness
no matter what the Circumstances, Conditions or Actions.

The aspirant is deeply moved and asks,
How do I ensure that I remain in continuous consciousness?

Your question shows me you are ready for a most important step.
This step involves what you are to learn

in this whole phase named
the Meditation of Action.

It is important for you to understand that, so far,
your response to the deepest inner urgings
has been incomplete.
Now, in the meditation of action, you learn what makes *real*
your relationship to the knowledge you have gained:
to not only be *aware* of your inner experiences,
but to *act* upon them.

You act as the royal Being acts:
living in the moment-to-moment Awareness
of limitless all-pervasive eternal Being that you are,
you express the Knowledge and Joy of infinite Self
through every Action.

Be focused,
for the greatest joys will now be revealed to you.

Deeply absorb this, says the guide to the aspirant:
the king does not *think* about *becoming* eternal,
but *acts* constantly in the *experience* of eternal Being.

For you to be real, for you to be in integrity,
your actions must come forth

from the consciousness of the Being you are.

You act strongly and clearly in the *expertise* you have gained,

faithfully—with trust in yourself—

and *continuously*—free of backsliding—

as the Self that you are.

In the meditation of action

you act as self-knowing, self-empowered, limitless Being.

Every action is a conscious and joyous expression of Being,

a celebration of what *is*.

Acting in the consciousness of Being

you deeply impress upon your mind, feelings, emotions

and the rest of your faculties

the experience of your limitlessness

in the conduct of your practical day-to-day life.

This is an important step on your path.

Do what you must in order to remember this. Now.

To be real, to be in Integrity,
have your Actions come forth from the Consciousness of Being
that you are.
Act strongly and clearly in the *Expertise* you have gained,
faithfully—with Trust in yourself—
and *continuously*—free of Backsliding—
as Self.

Act as self-knowing, self-empowered, limitless Being.
Every Action is a conscious and joyous Expression of Being,
a Celebration of what *is*.

Acting in the Consciousness of Being
you deeply impress upon your Mind, Feelings, Emotions
and the rest of your Faculties
the Experience of your Limitlessness
in the Conduct of your practical day-to-day Life.
This is an important Step on your Path.
Do what you must in order to remember this.
Now.

However, cautions the guide,

throughout the ages guides have discovered

that people are easily distracted

from the experience of themselves,

from the experience of what is.

The greatest distractions can be your activities.

Your activities—and the objects they involve—attract your mind.

That is why some guides claim

that actions are antithetical to the experience of Being:

they distract your mind's attention

and keep it riveted to the limitations

of the physical, sensual or mental realm.

As long as your mind is preoccupied

with fragmentary experiences,

you will tend to *not* be in awareness of the *wholeness* of Being,

the reality of you.

When your Mind is pre-occupied with fragmentary Experiences,
you will tend to *not* be in Awareness of the *Wholeness* of Being,
the Reality of you.

Thus there have been whole orders and schools

founded on the premise

of engaging in as little action as possible.

Participants employ others to perform their actions

so they can be inactive and therefore focused in wholeness.

Such teaching has you reject action

in a vain attempt to gain the experience of union with Being.

But there is a fundamental problem with that approach.

As human beings we cannot be without action.

Even if someone else does almost everything for us,

we still have to perform certain actions for ourselves,

like keeping the heart pumping—this is an action—

or the breath flowing,

or ingesting food,

even if someone else places it into your mouth.

Always remember this:

> To reject any Aspect of all-pervasive Being
> is to reject the limitless Oneness
> that is the fundamental Reality of Being.

The guide states with serious emphasis,

The significant question is:

how do you remain undistracted while engaging in activity?

The aspirant is puzzled.

Listen carefully, says the guide.

Here is a secret of profound importance for you:

the solution lies not in *rejecting* action,

but in *utilizing* all actions as opportunities

to express the Being you truly are

and thereby to continually *experience*
the reality that is the essence and identity of all.

> The Solution lies not in *rejecting* Action,
> but in *utilizing* all Actions as Opportunities
> to *express* the Being you truly are
> and thereby to continually *experience*
> the Reality that is the Essence and Identity of all.

When every action in your practical day-to-day conduct of life
is to you a joyous experience and expression
of self-knowing Being,
you are liberated from the negative effects of action—
from being distracted, limited and bound to the material realm.
It is good enough for the queen to be engaged in action;
why, then, should *we* reject it?

The aspirant understands this and is filled with joy.

Is this your attitude toward your actions?

The guide shares from his life:
There was a time when I found myself
living high above the world in the loftiest mountains
in a sacred cave on the banks of a great river.

The tranquility of life in this special place
was a drastic change from the busy life I led before.

I dwelled from dawn to dusk—day to day—wholly absorbed
in the experience of myself in pure consciousness.
It was time in the eternal continuum,
free of limits, deeply nurturing and satisfying.
Other than the few actions required
to maintain my material existence,
I had nothing to do but be in meditation.
The mountain dwellers provided for me,
considering it sufficient reward to have in their midst
someone abiding sincerely
in the luminous state of royal Being,
the state of meditation.

Absorbed in meditation,
I experienced consciousness as infinite,
beyond the reach of time or space.
Dwelling from morning to night in meditation,
the deepest joy radiated from my core
throughout and all around me
into complete flowing realization of limitless luminous Being.
I felt I could have joyously remained there forever.

However, while I savored being in this blissful freedom,
I was aware of those who suffer in the pits of murk and despair
because they do not know
how to be in such unencumbered experience

of the Being they, too, really are.

They are Being, just as I am,

yet their whole life is one of suffering.

They suffer because they know not who they are

and how to consciously live as all-pervasive power of Being.

So many of our fellow humans suffer so abjectly.

Most of their suffering is self-imposed.

This suffering is so needless;

it is not necessary and there is really nothing to be gained by it.

There is no advantage to it.

The guide states with calm emphasis,

Suffering is caused within.

Suffering is not caused by circumstances or conditions,

but by how we *respond* to them.

When we respond as isolated limited little ego, we suffer;

when we respond as the power of Being that we are,

we remain balanced and clear

irrespective of circumstances and conditions.

Suffering is caused within.

Suffering is not caused by Circumstances or Conditions,

but by how we respond to them.

When we respond as isolated limited little Ego,

we suffer;

when we respond as the Power of Being that we are,

we remain balanced and clear

irrespective of Circumstances and Conditions.

How about you, do you still suffer?

The guide continues,

> In awareness of Self,
>
> I am in awareness of my interconnectedness with all.
>
> Those who suffer due to lack of real self-knowledge
>
> are the same interconnected power of Being that I am.
>
> Thus it is *inherent* to me
>
> to want to share the experience of the joy of Being
>
> and the direct ways of attaining that state.
>
> How could I let them suffer
>
> when I knew how they could stop suffering?
>
> I had to come back.
>
> That is why I dedicate my life to functioning as a guide.

The cessation of suffering and living in the joy of real Being
    is relatively easy to achieve.

If I was able to achieve it, anyone is able to achieve it—
that is a fact.
But you have to be *sincere*,
you have to be *real* about it;
you cannot just fantasize,
you cannot merely wish or plan it.

Often People plan, I'm going to get myself together,
before I die, I'll get myself together.
Why wait that long
and have all those intervening Years in Suffering?
And how do you know you can focus
on realizing your Life-mission
while you are in the Crisis of Dying?

So, I relinquished my sanctuary in the mountain cave
to engage in the actions of serving as a guide
to the liberation from suffering.
The liberation from suffering takes place in individuals who,
through direct guidance from a *real* guide,
allow themselves the experience of being at home
in the realm of fulfillment,
the realm of reality, of Self.

> The Liberation from Suffering takes place in Individuals who,
> through direct Guidance from a *real* Guide,
> allow themselves the Experience
> of being at Home in the Realm of Fulfillment,
> the Realm of Reality, of Self.

To serve as guide is not some noble purpose for me,

>   but a simple response
>   to the awareness of our essential oneness.
>   How can we enjoy the experience of our oneness
>   while we abandon others to suffering?

While living in the cave, it was so clear to me

>   that fulfillment is simple, it is not at all complicated;
>   the complications we become enmeshed in
>   are due to the habit of self-limitation.

Living congruent with who we really are
directly results in a Life of Joy.
This is available to all.
The inevitable Consequences
of being congruent with ourselves are
Peacefulness and Vitality,
Release from Suffering.

The guide recalls,

At one moment I did feel a tug of opposition
to becoming busy again with all the *doing*.
But I said to myself,
'I can sit in this sacred place and be in eternal bliss,
but if I were to be in this balanced state of consciousness
while maintaining a household or even a family,
that would be a greater encouragement to others
to avail themselves of the life of their real identity.
Then my actions in interconnectedness
would encourage others.'

One who acts in the Awareness of Self
is a living Example to Others.

Do you conduct your actions in the awareness
        of your interconnectedness with all?

The guide calmly shares with his initiate,

        Thus I made a conscious decision to return to my active life,

        not as a sacrifice,

        but as an opportunity to express and share

        the experience of self-knowing interconnected Being

        that I am

        and that we all are.

As you can be in consciousness of limitless Being while in quietude,

        you can be in consciousness while in activity.

        However, you do have to make the decision

        to maintain your faculties in consciousness.

        It does not just happen by itself;

        you have to commit to it.

        And you have to fulfill that commitment rigorously, in reality.

        When you firmly and with full integrity commit yourself

        to engaging in every action as a way of expressing real Self,

        you will be in the continuous experience of consciousness.

        You will be amazed and delighted to find

        how everything about you cooperates in presenting to you

        a wealth of joy, ease, real success and fulfillment.

Being the real you is not to be regarded as merely a Practice,

something to engage in now and then;

it is to be enacted and lived continuously.

Remember the fundamental fact of your identity:

you are Being.

This is of such cardinal importance

that I will help you re-experience

what I have taught you before regarding your identity.

In essence you are Being; in reality—in fact—you are Being.

Being is not an organ or an object doomed to decay.

Being is the power by which you are,

the power *that* you are.

Power—as you have learned—is *indestructible* and *indivisible*.

That means power is infinite in time and space:

eternal and *all-pervasive*.

You are the power of Being.

Thus *you are* indestructible and indivisible,

eternal and all-pervasive.

Power is *indestructible* and *indivisible*.

That means Power is infinite in Time and Space:

eternal and *all-pervasive*.

You are the Power of Being.

Thus *you are* indestructible and indivisible,

eternal and all-pervasive.

I know you may find this hard to absorb, says the guide,

and again I remind you:

while you are not accustomed to thinking of yourself this way,

any other way of thinking is false.

Take heart, with my guidance

and through your own experience

you will become deeply familiar with this knowledge,

for it is inherent to you.

The pure energy that is the Self you are

is now,

has always been

and shall eternally be,

independent of time, space and circumstance.

Live in accord with that and you will be free and empowered.

This you will experience without doubt.

> The pure Energy that is the Self you are
>
> is now,
>
> has always been
>
> and shall eternally be,
>
> independent of Time, Space and Circumstance.
>
> Live in Accord with that and you will be free and empowered.
>
> This you will experience without Doubt.

Have you engaged with the teachings of this saga

as a focused experience in which you so sincerely remain

that you benefit from this freedom and empowerment?

The guide continues,

You cultivate familiarity with the knowledge of Self

by consistently engaging in all your actions

in the ways you are learning now in the meditation of action.

The meaning of every action

lies in the experience and expression of the Self you are.

Verily, the meaning of *being*

lies in the experience and expression of the Self you are.

The Meaning of every Action
lies in the Experience and Expression of the Self you are.
Verily, the Meaning of *being*
lies in the Experience and Expression of the Self you are.

Act consciously as the Being that you are;

thus you participate in—and contribute to—

the beauty of reality.

Do you recognize the special gifts that *you* can contribute

to the beauty and color of the royal realm?

Your distinctive characteristics,

such as your sincerity, your courage and your perseverance,

are what propelled you here

from the realm of murk and suffering.

Acknowledge your strengths,

treat them with respect and savor them.

They are integral to the beauty of Being.

Yes, says the aspirant to the guide,

to think of my strengths that way really helps.

However, when I think of actions, my mind distracts me.

What can I do about that?

The guide says,

Listen carefully, for I will tell you a great secret

about remaining focused while engaged in action:

> Whatever Action you are engaged in,
> have your Mind relate to it
> as a Way of being aware of Self.

In the realm of the meditation of action,

  you discover that all actions are, always have been
  and always will be
  performed by the one all-pervasive Being
  whom we call the king or queen of the realm.
  That is the unified Self.

Remember:

> There is one unified Self.
> The Perception of a separate self is but an Illusion.
> A separate self does not exist.

The guide clarifies,

  The false perception of separateness, isolation
  and fragmentation disappears
  when you experience the unified Self that we *all* are.
  Remember what you have learned:

the power of Being, like all power, is indivisible.

Nor does the perception of *separate agency* remain.

Since there is no separate Being,

there is no separate agent, no separate *doer.*

The separate agency of action is a false perception, ego.

Have you freed yourself from the false perception of separateness?

In the meditation of action we consciously act as the One we are.

Can you understand then,

how consciously acting as unified Being affects your actions?

Every one of your actions, as well as all your behaviors,

will be congruent with you,

therefore self-empowering and successful in reality.

You act as an expert acts.

Act as an Expert acts.

Furthermore, when performing an action,

you no longer say, 'I did a good job,'

thinking as the isolated ego.

You think, feel and act as infinite Being.

There is but one actor, one Being,

just as for each wave there is but one ocean.

> For each Wave there is but one Ocean.

The all-pervasive power of Being performs all actions
>   in the fluid ease and grace of knowing Self to be infinite,
>   in the delight of experiencing and expressing
>   the one Being that we are.
>   That is the meditation of action.
>   Meditation is the experience of Self—
>   the limitless Being that we are—
>   at will, free of distortion, distraction and interruption.
>   Thus:

> The Meditation of Action is
> performing Actions
> in the Experience of the limitless Being we are,
> at Will,
> free of Distortion, Distraction and Interruption.

The aspirant sincerely endeavors to experience these teachings,
>   for he knows he has been entrusted
>   with deeply significant knowledge.

The guide continues,

    To act as the infinite One is sufficient;

    it is enough for us.

    It is enough to be in the fluid ease of self-knowing experience

    gracefully expressed through our actions

    celebrating Being—all-pervasive and eternal.

    That is enough.

The aspirant smiles to himself

    for he recognizes the understatement.

In the meditation of action, his guide elaborates,

    you do not act to gain something.

    You simply act because eternal Being acts,

    independent of results.

You do not love someone to gain Love;

you simply love because of your limitless Interconnectedness.

You do not achieve Fulfillment

by acting in order to have Fulfillment;

you simply act as royal Being acts,

free of Attachment to the Fruits of Action.

Thereby you are fulfilled.

Everything is *within* royal Being,

    everything is *of* royal Being,

and everything *is* royal Being or manifestation thereof.

However, limitless Being is not contained in anything.

And remember, when you *are* all you *have* all,

thus there is no need.

Royal Being has no need to perform actions;

she merely acts in spontaneous pleasure and joy of Being.

When you experience yourself in the Interconnectedness of all,

you know you *are* all

therefore you *have* all,

thus there is no Need.

Regard the sun.

The sun performs much action.

It emits the light that nurtures life.

The sun attracts the waters out of the oceans,

purifies them,

deposits them again in clouds

that yield their abundance upon the earth as rain,

which in turn fills the rivers and streams,

which nurture the forests that clean our air

and feed the plants we eat...

Do you ask why the sun shines?

The sun shines because the sun shines.

Being acts because Being acts.

Thus, act as self-knowing limitless Being acts.

With the knowledge of who you are as your foundation,

you act in freedom from attachment,

undistorted by need,

therefore in purity and clarity.

This is the formula for real—lasting—success.

With the Knowledge of who you are as your Foundation,

you act in Freedom from Attachment,

undistorted by Need,

therefore in Purity and Clarity.

But, says the aspirant,

when I do something, I want to be successful.

How can I be unattached?

The guide replies,

Many have difficulty accepting

that *un*attachment fosters success,

not attachment.

Their thinking is, 'If I want something badly enough'—

attachment—'I will succeed.'

By success they mean achieving certain results.

The problem with that way of thinking is
that they are hitching the cart before the horse.

When you act in the consciousness of your real identity—
interconnected power of Being—
you act in pure self-experience and self-expression,
with all your faculties on the task,
undistracted by need and attachment,
therefore with ultimate focus and expertise.
Certainly you need not worry about results.
The fact that your actions are in harmony with reality
is enough.

When your actions are in harmony,
the results will be in harmony.
What more do you want?

> When your Actions are in Harmony,
> the Results will be in Harmony.

Observe children, for example, when they draw or paint.
They do so simply in the joy of action,
not to gain something.
If you praise them—
'What a great artist you are, what a beautiful picture'—
they shrink back.

You have interfered with their innocent spontaneity
by burdening them with your inclinations and expectations.
When you simply comment upon what you experience,
the children open to you and include you in their joy.
Gaining your praise should not be the goal of their actions;
it obliterates the real reward of their activities:
the pure pleasure of self-expression.

The guide faces the aspirant and speaks with emphasis:

> Action in Awareness of Being is its own Reward,
> for therein lies the Pleasure of Self-expression
> and Self-experience.

Actions are really for self-expression and self-experience.
Anything else is baggage to which people attach themselves
and thus deprive themselves of the highest reward.
This is typical in the land of murk:
throw out the essential and keep the superficial.
They do this even with meditation.
In the realm of illusion, it is popular to 'meditate'
in order to manifest material wealth:
'I meditated on getting a better job,'
'I meditated on scoring a goal' or '…winning a promotion'
or '…the lottery.'

They use the beautiful process of liberation
to create more material attachments,
thus more bondage to the ego.
Why would anyone insist on giving himself
such a shabby deal?

Ego protests, 'Do I have to be poor...?'
No, you do not have to be poor.
However, when you pervert the highest experience—
the experience of Being, absolute and eternal—
to obtain isolated objects,
you *insist* on being poor,
you short-change yourself!

The difficulty arises from living as a separate entity,
like a fragment that has been severed from the whole.
Then it seems difficult
to have no need for the results of actions.
A separate entity has enormous need:
to have and to hold,
to be connected and not isolated,
to perform action in order to achieve.
But you are not a separate entity.
Remember always, you are Being,
and all Being is infinitely interconnected.

The aspirant feels appreciation and apprehension:
I understand what you are teaching me here
and how significant it is.

However, I still have difficulty
letting go of my attachment to success.

The guide says patiently,

You may understand intellectually what I am teaching you
regarding attachment and failure,
as well as unattachment and success,
but you negate this understanding if you think,
'I know I am limitless Being,
but my knowledge is not valid
because I am not living true to who I am.'
Even if you live in utter contradiction to the Self you really are,
you still are Self.
Reality always persists,
whether you function in accord with it or in opposition.

> Reality is Reality whether you live in Accord with it or not.

So, do not discredit your intellectual understanding,
it can be a good start.
Live and act in integrity with what you intelligently know,
and your feelings, emotions—
all your instruments of experience—will come along.
Have you not noticed?

Impress this deeply:

>in the realm of reality, you do not attach yourself
>to the results of your actions,
>for there is no need.
>When you attach yourself to results,
>you are diverting energy onto the attachment
>instead of focusing upon the actions.

You too may choose to impress this deeply:

In the Realm of Reality, you do not attach yourself
to the Results of your Actions,
for there is no Need.
When you attach yourself to Results,
you are diverting Energy onto the Attachment
instead of focusing upon the Actions.

The guide speaks emphatically,

>Not being attached to results
>allows you to perform *perfect action.*
>Perfect action keeps you free
>of the binding consequences of action—
>the cycles of action and reaction
>that can occupy your energies endlessly.

Now, says the guide in a way that focuses the aspirant's attention,

what is perfect action?

Perfect action is any action

that is performed in consciousness of real Self.

Can you feel the depth of freedom this offers?

> Perfect Action is any Action
> performed in Consciousness of real Self.

The aspirant mentally repeats,

'Perfect action is any action

that is performed in consciousness of real Self.'

She impresses this wisdom deeply within.

Understanding dawns.

The guide continues,

There is another great benefit:

when you act as self-sufficient Being—

not attached to results—

you also are freed from the suffering of *procrastination*.

Due to procrastination you do not do what you intend

or want or even need.

You procrastinate because you mistakenly judge yourself

as inherently faulty.

Your irrational response to this erroneous thinking

is to demand that the results of your actions

be *inhumanly perfect.*

Aware of your inability to act with such perfection,

you are frozen in fear, you avoid acting.

Remember:

Procrastination is the Result of

mistakenly judging yourself as inherently faulty.

Impress this.

Eternal all-pervasive Being does not do things wrong.

When you know you are Being,

you need not worry about doing things perfectly.

Procrastination is an expression of distrusting yourself.

Action free of attachment is an expression of self-trust.

Action free of Attachment is Expression in Self-trust.

Procrastination is a powerful means to waylay yourself.

The fears and concerns involved in procrastination

dissipate your energy,

energy you could use to act directly,

focused in the Being that you are.
You need not fear:
when you act as the royal Being acts,
you are free from the results of action,
whatever they may be.
Besides, with your energies thus freed,
you naturally function more effectively.

You will learn to constantly relate to everything
      as wonderful ways of experiencing that you are,
      without concern about how it all ends up.
      The very accidents of life,
      or even the things you try to prevent,
      can yield unexpected benefits in life.

Trust in your eternal Beingness,
      trust that everything is contained
      within the limitlessness of Being.
      You are Being.

The aspirant asks,
      Does that not make me careless in my actions?

The guide replies,
      This attitude does not make you lackadaisical;
      it makes you focused
      because you do not waste energy worrying,
      you do not distract yourself with anticipation.

People often think it is responsible to worry
>
> and irresponsible to *not* worry.
>
> In which way are you really more able to respond successfully:
>
> when tied up with worry
>
> or when you have your faculties flowing freely?
>
> It is a subtle balance
>
> to be unconcerned while focused in expertise.
>
> This *is* the way to be effective.

Freedom from Worry comes from Trust in Self.

Do you trust in Self?

The aspirant now trusts that no matter what happens,
>
> he will be well.
>
> What a powerful and deeply comforting feeling.
>
> He remembers that all actions are performed by the One;
>
> all actions are the king's actions, the queen's actions.

His guide explains,
>
> Therein lies the secret of success
>
> and the key to overcoming our long-standing habit
>
> of resistance to action.
>
> In the awareness of *who* performs the actions
>
> you are true to real Being in self-expression.
>
> All actions are of the royal Being—that you are—

and those actions are performed without attachment to results
and without anxiety: without need, period.

Now you perform your actions in complete freedom.

In freedom you act consciously.

Consciously acting is assuming leadership of your life,

no longer allowing yourself to be victimized

by circumstances and conditions

or behavior patterns of the past.

It is being proactive.

You trust in the limitless intelligence

of the all-pervasive power of Being,

you trust in the intelligence of Self.

Again: success.

The freedom of non-attachment

allows you to act without encumbrance

and thereby in the limitless expertise that yields success.

Through *conscious action* you realize your liberation.

You are free from the false conceptions regarding your identity

that bind you to insecurity, fear, lack and need,

and all the resultant suffering.

Only in this freedom

are you able to realize lasting, vigorous joy—

not the superficial, momentary titillation of your senses,

which predictably yields disappointment,

but the deep-reaching joy in the power of Being that you are.

And the aspirant, being open, experiences the fullness of this joy.

In the murky realm,
>she suffered great hardship.
>She was always searching but never satisfied,
>always attempting but never successful.
>She wandered in circles of repetitive action
>that dug her deeper and deeper into the rut of misery.
>And where did this eventually land her?
>In the seemingly bottomless pit of despair and depression,
>anxiety and hopelessness.
>She sank into nearly total inability to move.
>You can spend years and years—even a lifetime—
>in that paralysis.

When you engage in superficial Actions
merely to maintain the material Plane,
you do not advance toward the Joy of real Self-experience;
you are stuck,
painfully and debilitatingly stuck.

The aspirant remembers how the actions
>to which she previously dedicated all her energy
>yielded no nourishment, no satisfaction or advantage.
>They drained her vitality and gave her nothing in return.

How horrible her life was then.

It was like eating food with no nourishment in it—

forcing her system to process the food and storing its toxins,

while deriving absolutely no benefit from the activity.

That is how she lived.

Now, in her newfound freedom of action,

she acts in sheer delight

and she acts with meaning.

The guide reminds her,

The meaning of your actions

lies in the experience and expression of the Being you are.

Why would anyone purposely perform actions

that deprive him of the experience of Being,

the fundamental experience that we seek

and for which we are in this life?

Now the aspirant knows that actions have the potential

to be expressions of Being

through which he can acknowledge

and thereby experience even more fully

the reality of limitless Self.

As a consequence, the more energy he expends in action,

the more energy does he gain, not lose.

The guide says,

When you act in accord with the meaning of your life—

in expression of Self—

to whom are you giving the energy of your actions?

Not to something outside yourself, but to you.

There *is* nothing outside yourself:

all actions are *of* you, *for* you, *by* you, infinite Self.

The doer and the action and the recipient of the action are one.

When you act as the Self you are,

the Doer,

the Action

and the Recipient of the Action

are one.

The energy you spend in actions

is not dissipated into something unknown,

some vast separateness or otherness;

you re-absorb that energy unto yourself.

Thus your actions nurture you.

Yes, says the aspirant,

in the past, my actions completely exhausted me.

There was nothing nurturing about that.

The guide acknowledges,

Your actions exhausted you because you were acting

in the false regard of yourself as a weak and separate entity.

You were not acting as self-knowing interconnected Being;

you were acting as a victim in the land of lack—
that *is* exhausting.

Actions performed in the consciousness of who you are,
rather than exhausting you, fulfill you:
they fill you with real pleasure.
What a release this is!
What joy! says the guide to the aspirant.
This is a fundamental and significant transformation,
which only you can bring about for yourself.

With great enthusiasm and vitality,
with openness and spontaneity,
the aspirant sincerely endeavors
to make this profound transformation
and become expert in acting in the awareness of Self—
in the meditation of action.
He knows this is the way to nurture himself, to fulfill himself.
This is what he has always sought in his actions.

Now the aspirant delights in action.
No longer does he see action as a burden or a duty;
he sees conscious action as deeply nurturing self-expression,
the most direct means of self-experience
wherein lie joy, empowerment and bliss.

I am the parent of sons, says the guide.
Through them I have learned much.
When my youngest son was little,

often, upon awakening in the morning

he would look at me, his face shining with joy, and say,

'Papa, let's play!'

All action was play for him and he delighted in play.

As he grew, his actions became more sophisticated.

By the age of three he wanted to act more like his parents,

so he thought that sweeping the floor, or writing,

or helping around the garden

were wonderful activities.

He still does not see those actions as work and thus repulsive.

It is a difference in perception.

Healthy children stay busy with actions all day long, until they drop.

And you wonder, 'Where do they get the energy?'

The more energy they expend,

the more energy they seem to gain,

much to the chagrin of parents

who are not in the same modality.

In the realm of suffering many have the attitude,

'I will start living when I am finished with work,'

or even, '…when I am retired.'

What happens to many after they retire?

They die soon after retirement

because they have no history of being in awareness of Self

and never learned how to live without being told what to do.

Their job is their reason for living.

At the same time, they resent work as a repulsive interference and regard action as an imposition.

This results in the loss of precious life experience.

The guide continues,

There are examples throughout nature

of how to act toward fulfillment.

Animals, for example, have wonderful ways

that show us how to act.

One of my great teachers was a dog.

He taught unconditional love, nobility and integrity in action.

He embodied those fine qualities throughout his life;

he never varied from his loyalty

and from an inherent goodness.

He was a noble being.

> The Enactment of your noble Qualities
> propels you toward Self-realization.

The aspirant is alert.

She determines to emulate the eternal king's way of acting.

She uses all her powers of observation to actually learn reality

so as to *live* reality,

not to *rationalize* falsity.

The guide says,

How does the king act?

The king, the power of Being

who is the all-pervasive essence of all,

is totally self-sufficient, therefore absolutely beyond need.

Thus, when the king acts,

he does not act because he *needs* to;

he chooses to act as an *example for humankind.*

If infinite Being chooses to engage in action,

then certainly it behooves us to do so.

Since we are in the sad habit of identifying ourselves by our bodies,

we experience ourselves bound to the forces of nature

of which inertia is one of the greatest and most influential.

Inertia is the tendency to continue in the same state

unless another and greater force causes a change.

Thus this powerful and persistent tendency resists growth—

growth is change—

and we know what happens to an organism that does not grow:

it perishes.

When inertia has a person resist developmental, emotional

or psychological growth, for example,

a deeply detrimental arrest takes place

in that person's life and evolution.

The person suffers extreme dysfunction,

a block to the inherent tendency to flourish.

It is due to inertia that we routinely repeat previous behaviors,

even if we first engaged in them long ago,

perhaps in childhood,

and even if we know they harm us.

Thus many of our behaviors are motivated

by habitual patterns and tendencies,

not by our adult and informed choice.

Our perceptions, choices and behaviors of childhood

are not always the most successful for our life as adults.

Our Perceptions, Choices and Behaviors of Childhood

are not always the most successful for our Life as Adults.

The aspirant worries,

> Since inertia is such a powerful force to keep things the same,
>
> it is not surprising that so many of us suffer so much
>
> due to our resistance to growth.
>
> I have seen it in myself so often.

The guide warmly regards the initiate:

> It is already to your advantage
>
> that you are able to notice and admit to yourself
>
> this tendency to resist growth.
>
> However, you *have* grown in leaps and bounds
>
> since you committed to live true
>
> to the Being that you now know you are.
>
> I applaud you for responding
>
> to all the knowledge you have gained in these realms

from the many experiences through which I have guided you.
Your response has *not* been mere learned words,
nor just wishing and wanting and making commitments,
but you have persistently taken action to oppose the attachment
to the inertia caused by past conditioning.
Choosing actions according to your knowledge
and persistently applying those chosen actions
frees you from the bondage to inertia and its inevitable result:
suffering in dysfunction and arrested development—failure.

Choosing Actions according to your Knowledge
and persistently applying those chosen Actions
frees you from the Bondage to Inertia and its inevitable Result:
suffering in Dysfunction and arrested Development—Failure.

So you see, smiles the guide, you need not worry.
Do you remember what I just told you about inertia?
Inertia is the tendency to continue in the same state
unless another and greater force causes a change.
You have already proven
your ability to apply the force that opposes inertia!
That is why you have progressed on your path so successfully.
You are engaging in the behaviors of an adult knowing Being,
true to yourself and empowered.

Sincerely and persistently continue in this manner
with the expertise you are gaining
and with trust in Self that you are,
and nothing will interfere with your glorious success
in gaining the core of the realm of fulfillment.
Of this be assured.

The initiate feels uplifted,

for she experiences directly
what the guide has pointed out so enthusiastically.

The guide elaborates,

As long as you were enslaved by inertia,
your life was stuck in a rut
and persistent suffering alerted you to the situation.
The king, in his abiding love, shows us positive action
in order to help us overcome inertia and thereby thrive.
We have to take action, as you have learned.
We act not only to maintain our physical vehicle,
but also to advance on our evolutionary path:
to reach the highest level of consciousness
in which we experience ourselves continuously and in reality
as the imperishable, all-pervasive,
conscious power of Being.

We act not only to maintain our physical Vehicle,
but also to advance on our evolutionary Path:
to reach the highest Level of Consciousness
in which we experience ourselves in Continuity and Reality
as the imperishable, all-pervasive,
conscious Power of Being.

Thus, says the guide, act as the king acts.

The king acts in the constant awareness of himself
as the all-pervasive essence,
the Self of all.
He acts in purity: free of desire for the fruits of action
and devoid of the sense of ego-doership.
Act in purity and you shall thrive.
Pure actions keep your mind undistracted,
for you perform them in reason, proper discrimination
and self-control.

> The Queen acts in the constant Awareness of herself
> as the all-pervasive Essence,
> the Self of all.
> She acts in Purity: free of Desire for the Fruits of Action
> and devoid of the Sense of Ego-doership.
> Act purely as Self and you shall thrive.

What results when you are focused in conscious actions
        sincerely, faithfully and continuously?
        Those actions advance you on your path to fulfillment
        more directly and easily than any other means.
        You experience yourself as totally interconnected, eternal,
        all-pervasive, conscious Being.

> Conscious Actions advance you on your Path to Fulfillment
> more directly and easily than any other Means.
> You experience yourself as totally interconnected, eternal,
> all-pervasive, conscious Being.

The aspirant repeatedly learns
        to act in the awareness of her real identity,
        in simplicity and directness,

in purity and clarity.

She learns through her close and honest relationship

with the guide,

and most of all, by observing his actions.

She changes her behaviors

and makes quantum steps of advancement.

She also observes how the king expresses himself

through everything in the realm:

not only through his higher functions as royal Being,

such as acting through the guide,

but also through the most mundane day-to-day activities.

She sees and feels the king

as every person and every part of the realm.

She learns quickly.

She *knows* the king, she *experiences* the king,

she merges with the king in her own experience.

The king is self-knowing.

The king constantly acts in the knowledge that he has all.

He *is* all.

Thus the king acts neither out of need nor out of lack,

neither out of competition nor out of isolation.

He acts in the pure bliss of self-experience

through all actions self-expressed.

> Be self-knowing.
> Constantly act in the Knowledge of Self.
> As Self you have all,
> you *are* all.
> Thus act neither from Need nor from Lack,
> neither from Competition nor from Isolation.
> Act in the pure Bliss of Self-experience
> through all Actions self-expressed.

As the aspirant endeavors sincerely and expertly

to act as the king acts—

in freedom, in joy and benevolence—

he discovers the deep *pleasure* of service.

In the realm of murk,

service was only for poor people from across the border,

for those who could not get good jobs.

Such servants did not like to perform service.

The aspirant is utterly amazed to learn

that in the royal realm the most active servant is the king:

the king himself is the servant of servants.

The king has claimed service unto himself

as the highest privilege.

He knows that service—

acting in the consciousness of interconnectedness—
is fulfillment in the experience of Being.

> Service—
>
> acting in the Consciousness of Interconnectedness—
>
> is Fulfillment in the Experience of Being.

The aspirant realizes that ego,
    which he had previously thought was his identity,
    does not see service as a privilege and a boon.

Yes, responds his guide,
    ego will not, cannot, see it this way;
    ego is of isolation.
    Ego does not experience service
    as the expression of unified Self.
    Due to its sense of separateness,
    the ego causes the perception of need
    and the illusion of limitedness and weakness.

You cannot expect the ego to agree to the boon of service,
    because ego is the product of false conception
    and does not conceive the reality of interconnected Being.
    In fact, ego finds every possible excuse to contradict reality.
    Your experiences in reality expose the falsity of ego.

Ego is skilled in making fancy rationalizations

    to prevent your participation in service.

    The ego uses even your aspirations

    to be in the awareness of Self,

    to rationalize *not* being in Self.

    The ego claims holiness,

    'For the sake of my advancement in Self-realization,

    I must not do such a lowly thing as service,'

    or, 'I have to keep things balanced, service is too challenging.'

Ego will even advance such self-contradictory thinking as,

    'I do not have time to be me.

    I have more important things to do,

    things that have nothing to do with me.

    For my own sake, I must not have authority imposed upon me

    by being told to work in an organized and unified way

    as infinite Being.

    I must maintain my autonomy.'

    You could translate this as,

    'For the sake of my dominance,

    I must remain isolated in ego separateness

    and its despairing and disorganized activities.'

    Nobody would ever say this openly,

    yet internally this is often the response.

    Service frightens the ego more than anything,

    because service is the experience of Self in self-expression.

One day the aspirant finds herself standing with her guide
    at a beautiful pristine beach.
    To make clear the relationship of the individual
    to the all-inclusive power of Being,
    the guide shares with her the analogy of the ocean wave.

Acting as the real Self, he says,
    you act with an understanding of your abundance,
    you act without need;
    you act as a way of expressing interconnectedness
    with all your manifestations;
    you serve your infinite self-expressions in all your actions—
    you are like the ocean who constantly serves every wave
    and every creature within her.

Imagine the wave thinking, 'I have to be a wave; I am not the ocean.
    My individuality, my existence,
    depends on me being a separate wave;
    merging with the ocean is the end of me.
    I fear the ocean.'
    It is easy to see the falsity in that.

The guide then offers her a spontaneous experience
    of the relationship of herself to the whole,
    of the wave to the ocean:

Feel free to experience this along with the aspirant.

A Wave
I am a Wave, a Wave.

She expressed me
from deep within her Loins,
my Mother, the Ocean,
and flung me forth
upon her endless frothy Breast.
A Wave
I am a Wave, a Wave.

I have grown into my Form
and play and fight
with the Others
as I become more distinct,
myself.
A Wave
I am a Wave, a Wave.

As I rear myself proudly above the Ocean
I forget my Source,
and I move ever further
through glittering hot Day
and through star-spangled Night
as I cry out my Loneliness.
A Wave
I am a Wave, a Wave.

On one dark turbulent Night
I rear up in Fright
when I see myself hurtling heedlessly
toward the sharp-rocked Shore.
I know my Fate
as I see Others before me
dashed to Oblivion
against unyielding Stone.
A Wave
I am a Wave, a Wave.

I helplessly dash onward
to my Annihilation
in the Frenzy of Fear,
which at last I bring to Stillness.
I meet jagged and round Rock
and give up my Form
of the Wave,
the Wave, that Wave.

I immerse myself again
in the cooling Depth
of Mother Ocean
and realize that
I am That.
I am the infinite Ocean
I am That
I am, I am.

Can you imagine, asks the guide, the wave fearing the ocean?
How silly that would be, how false.

<blockquote>
Ego is as silly and false as the Wave thinking of itself
as separate from the Ocean.
</blockquote>

Like the isolated wave, ego thinks,
'If I were to become the ocean
and therefore, as the guide says, the main servant of all,
how could I compete anymore?'

The aspirant acknowledges another concern:
From early on we are taught to think,
'If I were to function as a servant,
it would make me lower and weak,
and I would have to take from others
to gain stature and strength.'

Yes, says the guide,
that is the ignorance of ego.
The egotistical way of thinking
does not permit you the experience
of being the all-inclusive ocean of Being
who has no need.
Ego is so opposed to learning this,

the more real the teaching, the more the ego fights it—
again, because reality exposes ego's falsity.

> Ego is opposed to Learning.
> The more real the Teaching, the more Ego fights it.
> Reality exposes Ego's Falsity.

Our ego must learn how to transcend itself,
 for it too is invited to partake in the transformation.
 Originally, ego is simply the awareness of one's existence;
 you may regard ego as the 'I am' function, in the pure sense.
 However, most individuals modify ego into the
 'I am such-and-such' sense
 and thereby introduce all the false identification,
 which includes,
 'I am this body, an isolated entity
 dwelling in a vast interconnected cosmos,
 separate and so small as to be relatively insignificant;
 therefore I need and I fear and I am basically lonely.'
 Need, fear and loneliness are the results in life
 based on false perceptions
 attached to the modifications of the ego-sense.

What do you experience now? asks the guide.

The aspirant lights up with understanding:
>   I now can see how, before I met you,
>   I based my whole life, all my thoughts and actions
>   and even my feelings and emotions,
>   upon this modification of ego
>   that was founded upon a false perception regarding *who I am*!
>   Yes, and even my intellect was in service to this falsity.

The aspirant feels empowered, freed
>   and flooded with the light
>   of deeply experienced understanding:
>   I see, I really, really see!
>   Now I am free and will only live and breathe and think
>   and feel and act as the Being I am.

Consciously acting as the Power of Being that you are
is the most powerful and most direct Means
to *realizing* who you are,
thereby gaining your Fulfillment in Self-realization.

The guide feels the joy of the aspirant's realization.
>   He expresses a caution:
>   What is the *opposite* response?
>   *Knowing* reality but not *enacting* it—
>   just mouthing the words,

going through the motions,

fooling yourself with theories.

That is hypocrisy and rank foolishness,

for it deprives you of all you want and need

while deceiving you with the illusion

that you are actually doing it.

If you have difficulty relating to yourself

as the limitless power of Being that you *know* you are,

start *acting* that way, consciously.

Then you will no longer squander your energies—

your life experience and expression—

on illusion, falsity, on something that does not exist.

The guide offers the aspirant an experience:

Experience this now.

Imagine learning to consistently relate to yourself

with unconditional acceptance,

with limitless honor and respect, and utter love

as the interconnected power of Being that you know you are.

In relating to yourself this way,

you are blessed with great benefits,

such as living free of fear and lack

and all the accompanying suffering;

you are enriched with deep inner joy and security,

self-love and trust,

confidence, ease and success

in your workings and relationships,
as well as a wealth of lasting harmony, satisfaction and peace.

Now, knowing that you really are interconnected Being,
you really want to share your wealth
of knowledge and experience
so that other aspects of Being
benefit as you have.

Yes, says the aspirant, I feel that deep in my core.
I want to share the love and the light
and the knowledge of Self I have gained from you.
I want to be as generously giving and loving
as you have been to me.
You have constantly shown me by your example
how interconnected Being just gives.

> Interconnected Being gives
> to maintain Equality among all Parts.

The guide regards the initiate lovingly:
It is good for you to experience that feeling.
However, what have you *tended* to do?
Your tendency has been to run away
from the opportunity to really give to others—
as fast as you can—

and destroy it in your wake
to make sure it never threatens your ego again.

The aspirant has learned, though,
to resort to his knowledge, rather than his tendencies,
as the impetus for his actions.
He remembers how his tendencies
have led him into dysfunction and failure.

He understands also that knowledge alone is not enough.
He has to grow into the full experience of his real identity
by absorbing himself in the experience of interconnectedness.
He can only grow into the experience of interconnectedness
by functioning as all-pervasive Being does.

The Experience of being one all-pervasive Being is attained only
by acting as the royal Being acts.

Now the aspirant looks for opportunities
to involve himself in service
so he can emulate the queen, emulate his guide
and be, thereby, in the blissful experience
of Self in the unitive state.

And do you know what he finds?
His disdain for service has vanished.

He has a natural tendency to delight in service—
and he experiences this as wonderful!
He recognizes that he is not giving himself up through service;
the only thing he sacrifices is the falsity of ego
and the accompanying dysfunctions.
He gains deep satisfaction
and learns that service is its own reward.

> Service is its own Reward.

She understands that seeking rewards for service—
    recognition, money, gratitude, goods—
    limits the *real* benefits she accrues through her actions.

She acknowledges:

> Performing selfless Service
> without Desire for Rewards
> yields the highest Benefits.

She notices, when she engages in service her guide does not thank her.
    Earlier, this annoyed her;

she had to be recognized, appreciated and praised;
she wanted the guide to be grateful for what she did.
Now she recognizes that the guide honors her
by *not* thanking her.
How could this be?

The guide relates to the aspirant's actions
as he does to the king's actions,
as natural self-expressions
of interconnected self-knowing Being,
not as some honor the guide bestows upon her;
it is what she inherently deserves.
This is an important lesson in self-appreciation.
If the actions were bestowed upon the aspirant by the guide,
the aspirant would have to thank the guide,
and upon the tasks' completion
the guide would have to thank the aspirant.

Now, whenever the aspirant serves,
he knows he is serving different aspects of infinite Being
that in essence and reality he *is*.
He finds himself wonderfully relaxed in his actions,
at ease and relieved of anxiety.
Through service he experiences Being,
he experiences interconnectedness,
and he knows he belongs.
He knows he belongs.
Now he is even more freed from the perception of isolation.

His actions are fluidly effortless and successful.

He is an *expert in action.*

She feels in touch with the essence that she is

and no longer gives energy to suffering

by which she beleaguered herself in the past.

She lets go of the negativity of needless suffering

and does not reinvigorate and reinvent it.

And so our friend grows with these lessons.

This is not to say that everything happens smoothly

or that he accomplishes everything overnight.

He still faces challenges with egoless service now and then.

But he learns even more deeply not to fear his problems

or shun them,

nor is he repulsed by them:

he appreciates them as instruments for his advancement.

Her problems cease to be problems.

She appreciates 'problems'

as challenges to her new strength and confidence

by which she revels in her power to apply her skills to succeed

as self-knowing and confident Being.

Under the tutelage of her guide, she recognizes problems

as opportunities to open up into more expansive understanding

and deepening levels of awareness of Being.

She learns to convert obstacles

into steppingstones to higher realization.

This contributes greatly to her freedom.

> Regard 'Problems' as Challenges
> to exercise your Strength and Self-confidence
> and revel in your Power to apply your Skills to succeed
> as self-knowing and confident Being.
> Learn to convert Obstacles into Steppingstones to higher Realization,
> and thus contribute greatly to your Freedom.

How powerful this is! exults the aspirant.

> Now she no longer worries about *not* being worried.
> Worry used to be her familiar state,
> and she feared something was amiss when she was not worried.
> This, too, she is free of now.
> She trusts that whatever happens on her path to fulfillment
> she can relate to with equanimity,
> and thus it will be for the good.
> Her thoughts, feelings and actions
> no longer relate to the ego as her identity.
> She feels connected and alive
> through her empowered experience in egoless service.

The aspirant finds herself fully absorbed in the realm of Being,

> in the all-inclusiveness of Being.
> She feels inspired and learns to trust this inspiration
> as a powerful motivating force.
> Before, negativity was her motivating force.

It was only when she felt the abject misery

caused by all the negativity

that had landed her in the pit of despair,

that she gathered her energies and scrambled out.

The aspirant feels in touch with herself now

and resolves to give herself the pleasure

of responding to *inspiration*,

not to *suffering*,

as her motivating force.

Sincerely absorbed in service,

he finds that the meditation of action

is a most powerful lesson in transformation

that he looks forward to using fully.

He is excited by the potential.

It is clear to him now that he gains limitless power

when he claims the eternal realm of Self

through egoless service,

when he engages sincerely in acting like the king,

the number one servant.

The initiate, deeply moved by these lessons,

learns to love the guide even more:

their energies increasingly reverberate together.

This is a closeness she never experienced before.

She is learning to be in real relationship.

The aspirant openly states her gratitude

for how the guide so steadily relates to her:

with respect and warmth and kindness.
Thus begins within her a subtle movement—
like the unfolding of a lotus blossom—
that emulates the guide's deeply pleasing ways of being
by which she is so nurtured.

She feels an upsurge of joy and appreciation
for the pleasure of Being in which she now dwells
and with which she now identifies.
She learns to treasure the profound benefit
of acknowledging the deep satisfaction of experiencing Self.
This uplifting experience
is a source of increasing vitality and empowerment,
and a great boost to her trust in Self.

To help her grow
the guide challenges the aspirant with tasks to perform.
He gives her assignments
that aid her expansion into egolessness
and therefore self-trust.
With these experiences she grows more secure
in her understanding of her innate limitlessness
and thereby her full empowerment.

For example, one day the guide asks the aspirant
to plant five trees in the orchard
on ground that is rocky and hard.
The aspirant works with great effort
until he has blisters on his hands.

When he proudly shows off his planted fruit trees,
the guide tells him that he feels this is not quite the right place
and asks him to change the placement of the trees.

The aspirant notices within himself some annoyance,
but he faithfully replants the trees
and is amazed when the guide tells him it still is not right
and to please change the placement again.

By now, she is weary of the job;
she wants to savor her accomplishment.
However, she decides to see what happens;
she replants once more.

And would you believe it,
three more times the guide tells her
to change the placement of the trees in that rocky ground.
By the sixth planting,
the trees end up inches away
from where she had first planted them.

Now the aspirant finds herself ablaze with anger and consternation.
She knows the guide is wrong this time.
If her guide had his head on his shoulders correctly
and figured out what he wanted at the beginning,
the whole job would have been much faster, easier
and more satisfying.
So the aspirant says to herself,
Now I have 'one-up' on the guide,

and that alone is the saving grace
of this whole annoying experience.

Then, just a few moments later,

he recognizes the guide gave him this activity

to challenge the ego,

because the ego is the source of all despair,

the anchor to the realm of murk.

Through ego he reacted in the typical way:

becoming angry and frustrated,

accusing the guide of pressuring him,

boring him,

mistreating him.

He had failed to be in the *experience* of Being

while performing his actions

and thereby lost the opportunity

to be in the continuous *expression* of Being

while engaged in the mundane activity of planting trees.

The guide repeats his lesson of unattachment to the fruits of actions,

and the aspirant recognizes he forgot again.

He fell into the trap of performing his actions

as a wanderer from the realm of murk.

He was attached to having a good utilitarian purpose

for his actions;

he forgot to take pleasure in his actions,

to act in the consciousness of self-sufficient Being.

There is pleasure in actions
    when you recognize them to be expressions
    of the limitless Being that you are.
    She was delaying the pleasure to the future
    when the action would be completed.
    You must never delay or forsake the experience of Self
    for some future time.

> In the infinite Continuum of Time
> there is no Action for some future Result.

Thus the guide, risking the aspirant's displeasure,
    generously shows her
    how she failed to take pleasure in the actions
    as expressions of the one Being that she is;
    how she did not act as the queen acts;
    how she failed to experience her actions
    as the king's self-expressions,
    the one Being's self-experience.

The guide showed her that she forgot what she had learned.
    He points out,
    This is an important lesson:
    you may have the tendency to forget what you learn
    and thus continue acting as if you had not learned.

> You may have the Tendency to forget what you learn
> and thus continue acting as if you had not learned,
> acting in Ignorance.

The aspirant is sincere and the lesson takes hold quickly.
> He appreciates the invaluable understanding gained
> through the exercise of planting the trees.
> Before, he might have brooded, What does this mean?
> I am always wrong, and the guide is always right?
> He can tell me what to do but I cannot tell him what to do?
> The aspirant remembers
> that competitiveness distracts from the issue at hand:
> the gift and care he is actually receiving.

He grows with his new vision,
> even if sometimes he finds the actions of the guide
> difficult to understand or accept—
> or even if they stimulate his ire.

Have you ever noticed feeling ire
> *when someone supports you to Self-realization?*

The aspirant has advanced in trust—
> not only in the guide,
> but, more importantly, in herself.

The guide gives the aspirant another lesson
>   in trust and egoless service:
>   One day he asks the aspirant to go
>   where the privileged members of the royal realm
>   are frolicking on the beach.
>   The guide says to her,
>   Get a stick with a nail in the end of it
>   and walk through the crowd picking up their trash.

The aspirant immediately feels anger flare up:
>   I have advanced too far to go back to such menial tasks;
>   this is below my station.
>   And for a moment,
>   she is back in the ego realm of murk.

But then he catches himself;
>   he dismisses that thought
>   and endeavors to act as the king would act.
>   His experience is transformed into a beautiful one.

Later, on his way back from the beach
>   he sees people merrily throwing their trash
>   where he had just cleaned,
>   and this time he feels justifiably annoyed and unappreciated.

Again, in the flare-up of ego,
>   the habit of thinking of himself as a member of the gray realm
>   has re-asserted itself.
>   He is still attached to the fruits of his actions.

However, he is quicker at catching himself now.
He has learned to overcome the pride of ego.

> To be humble is not to lower yourself,
> but to heighten the Experience of Self,
> to go beyond Ego.

He marvels at the simple wisdom of his guide
and acknowledges himself
for having the good *uncommon* sense
to trust in his guide and to trust in himself.
Even though his old tendencies flare up now and again,
he will sincerely prevail over them.

The aspirant is aware of how frequently she has slipped backward,
as if she did not know better.
She makes a strong determination to not allow this anymore.

How do I ensure that I actually gain by what I learn?
she asks her guide.

The guide simply says,
Learn from your learning experiences.
Function in accord with the growth you have attained.

Learn from your learning Experiences.

Function in Accord with the Growth you have attained.

Through repetition, she deeply absorbs these lessons of egoless service
     and enacts them to advance herself
     on the path to enlightenment.
     They liberate her from the ways of being that yield pain,
     and she highly treasures them.
     These are the most powerful, essential lessons
     she has learned so far:
     they propel her most directly into the experience of joy,
     for through egoless action
     she becomes more intimately conscious
     of the all-pervasive Being that she is.
     The teachings are not mere words for her,
     but actual experience.

Thus, *action in the awareness of Being*—conscious action—
     is the most powerful propelling force
     by which he frees himself of the domination,
     indeed the slavery, of his tendencies
     and the habits that bound him to the past
     and his life in the realm of murk.

So now our aspirant becomes a super-servant,
     emulating the king,

emulating his guide.
Like the king, he functions as a principal servant
who acts out of the sheer delight
of experiencing and expressing Being
and thereby celebrates the interconnectedness of all his aspects.

Like the queen,
    she is not giving of herself to someone or something else—
    there *is* no one else,
    for all is the limitless power of Being,
    all is the queen.
    Giving *of* Self, she is giving *to* Self.

Newly sensitive to her inner experiences,
    she notices a subtle but persistent signal
    of something still lacking,
    and it puzzles her.
    However, by now she has learned to trust the voice within,
    to sit with her experience and observe without attachment
    and not to distract herself
    with judging her signals as wrong or right.

She discovers what is tugging at her:
    the memory of her fellow beings
    in the realm of suffering and lack.
    Suddenly she recognizes,
    This is the first time
    I am actually considering the people in the murky realm.
    My perception was so clouded when I dwelled there

that I felt and lived as if I were totally alone.
Her separateness had kept her encased in a thick wall
that she had built at great expense to her life;
she had lived in isolation,
virtually insensitive to the lives of others,
as if they did not exist.

Now that she is aware of her fellow beings in the gray realm,
    she knows they are still suffering,
        for they have not received guidance into the realm of plenty
        or enjoyed the benefits that she already takes for granted:
        being in touch with who she really is,
        being in agreement with herself,
        being free of despair and hopelessness
        and having a strong sense that all is possible
        and available to her.
    She now goes through life successfully,
        with vibrancy and hope,
        confidence and joy.
    To hoard all this positive experience
    and keep it secret for herself
    would be to regress to the egotistical behaviors
    that were familiar to her in the loneliness of the barren realm.

To continue in isolation in spite of all she has gained
        while traversing the realms of knowledge
        and the science of Self
        and now the meditation of action,

would contradict the knowledge she has gained.

Living in the sense of isolation

opposes herself

and her path toward fulfillment in the core of the royal realm.

This is now utterly clear to her,

yet she does not know what to do next.

He needs to respond to the inner urge to act in accord

with his awareness of interconnectedness in Being—

to share what he has gained—

but he does not know how to do so effectively.

Effectiveness has become an important concept to him.

He has gained enough respect for himself

that he wants to act expertly,

as does the queen.

With sincerity and trust,

the initiate appeals to the guide for counsel.

The guide applauds her for the insight that has led her to ask.

He says unto her, Let me assure you,

as you come closer to the very core of the royal court,

I will help you find the ways to fulfill the innate yearning

for effectiveness in action.

From my own experience I can tell you,

there will come a time when you will know

that to share your wealth of self-experience

is to propel yourself most immediately toward

the delight and deepest satisfaction your life yearns for.
Not to share is to deprive yourself.

She understands now,

the lonely emptiness she felt in the land of murk
was only her unrequited yearning to be here,
in this fullness of self-experience,
the experience of interconnectedness.
She achieves the final steps of her journey
by *enacting* her interconnectedness,
helping others from the realm of murk and darkness
into the realm of all.

Our aspirant delights in her growth,

which is increasingly effortless and joyous.
She delights in the expansiveness of her experience
and becomes truly wealthy,
not in material gains, which she no longer needs,
for she has all—she has the kingdom of eternal Being—
but she gains in the power and ability to dwell
in the very core of the royal realm.

From his guide he has learned deeply and well about service;

most of all, he has learned about service
from the *example* of the guide.
Though obviously belonging
to the realm of fulfillment and ease,
his guide unstintingly gives of his life and energy,

of his experience and unswerving love
to wanderers in the land of murk.

Through the example of the guide
and the knowledge gained from his own experience,
the aspirant now sees that his life has *meaning*.
He can consciously conduct his life in accord with its meaning
and no longer waste it in meaningless meandering.
It is an important recognition to him
that now he can dedicate his life to making a difference
and leave a positive mark on humanity.

Are you conducting your life in accord with its meaning?

The initiate looks forward
to more exercises and teachings from her guide—
challenges that she now sees as gifts.
More importantly,
the aspirant sees the opportunity of egoless service
as an expression of the guide's trust
in her loyalty to her knowledge and to herself.
The guide trusts in her ability to develop and expand
on her path to Self-realization.
The guide would never present her with challenges
she is incapable of meeting.

Infinite Being does not give us anything
for which we are not ready.
Remember this.
The more you are challenged,
the more you have earned Trust in your Abilities.

The aspirant savors what she has gained.

More and more she experiences her actions

as the king's actions;

she regards everything that happens here

as the queen's happening—

be it a mere word that comes forth from the aspirant's mouth,

a thought she has,

a feeling she experiences

or a deed she performs,

all are the king's queen's thoughts, feelings, deeds.

She recognizes the king in every aspect of the royal realm,

in every manifestation,

in every guise.

The king merely disguises himself, for whatever reason—

maybe just for the fun of it,

for his own eternal entertainment.

Her travels have at times seemed to cause her turmoil and resistance—

at least that is how she saw it.

Now, in retrospect, she realizes
her journey has been deeply nurturing and enjoyable.
All the things the aspirant has gone through
have turned out to be beautiful instruments of self-discovery
and transformation.

The aspirant recognizes he is free now from the feeling
that made everything seem gray and murky,
even at times the act of traversing the royal realm
with all the challenges and lessons.
Now he sees every experience
as part of the process of self-revelation.
He has let his increased knowledge
bring about increased internal development
by which he has significantly changed his behaviors,
his response to life and to his Being.
He is no longer *waiting* to be fully and forever
in the queen's realm,
as he recognizes he already *is* in the queen's realm.
All *is* the royal realm.

Thus the aspirant is empowered to advance directly
to the next gate.
Confident and deeply at ease in the company of the guide
and in heightened awareness of Self,
the aspirant approaches the fourth gate...

GATE FOUR

LOVE AND DEVOTION

Experience deeply, pay close attention.
> *Let us continue together on our journey.*
> *Be real, be focused and present.*
> *Sincerely participate in this experience*
> *as a direct way to effect your transformation.*

The aspirant easily enters
> and learns joyously and deeply
> of the realm of love and devotion.

She discovers that the great generous king,
> the queen of all that is,
> the royal Being of the limitless wholeness,
> has always been watching over her.
> Eternal Being has always been there for her,
> in touch with her,
> guiding her.
> The king of infinity has helped the aspirant
> in simple, humble ways,
> in service.

As the aspirant recognizes this,

>   she weeps tears of joy and gratitude.

Even when he was meandering aimlessly

>   in the realm of murk where he saw nothing but gray—
>   painting everything gray with his own eyes—
>   the queen of the luminous realm had been there for him.

It was the king who gave her the gift of the initial vision

>   of the colorful realm of fulfillment
>   that inspired her with the hope and strength
>   to struggle out of the pit of despair.

It was the queen who gave him the inspiring vision

>   every step of the way
>   to attract him to his salvation
>   and awaken him toward self-recognition,
>   to empower him to leave behind the land of non-being
>   to which he was so attached
>   and to find himself worthy to claim the beauty and grandeur
>   of the Being that he is.

She is amazed at royal Being's devotion to her,

>   and thus she is deeply moved into devotion to royal Being,
>   devotion to Self.

He remembers how lovingly the queen gazed upon him

>   when he first came to the royal realm
>   and the gates were flung wide open.

He feels a magnificent opening up

       as he recognizes that the plain-looking person,

       the inconspicuous one he first saw as a laborer

       and then petitioned to be his guide,

       is none other than the king himself

       in yet another disguise.

The guide is the king

       in the guise of *self-knowing* Self.

       The wanderer was the king

       in the guise of separate and *not-knowing* self.

It dawns upon the aspirant now with complete clarity

       that the all-pervasive power of Being,

       the absolute power of love,

       has always been his one refuge,

       the one he could always depend upon.

And all her yearning—

       whether she thought it was for food or security

       or sensual enjoyment,

       for closeness or love,

       for objects or conditions—

       was always for *union* with this beautiful,

       most benevolent loving power,

       the infinite royal absolute Being.

       She always yearned for this.

Now that she is in the queen's realm,

>   the aspirant sees how frequently her actions led
>   to the opposite of the pleasure and bliss that she sought
>   and that she now sees beckoning.
>   She understands something that is important to her:
>   because of actions opposite to who she is,
>   she lived in the conviction of her unworthiness—
>   not because she was unworthy.

The guide teaches her more about self-worth:

>   It has been said about you many times that you are unworthy,
>   as if it were true,
>   as if it were a given.
>   You were told that you come into this life with original sin,
>   stained.
>   And you spent much of your life fulfilling the prophecy—
>   self-fulfilling prophecy—
>   trying to prove the truth of this falsity.

But when you are adult,

>   who causes the perception of unworthiness?
>   Not the world,
>   not any outer authority,
>   but *you* do by your own self-negating behaviors.

The guide continues with loving focus:

>   When you feel unworthy,
>   it is not because someone made you feel unworthy.
>   Whenever you think negativity is coming from someone else,

first examine whether you are creating it.

Nobody can make you feel unworthy

when you are in touch with who you are.

Their negativity is their problem, their weakness, their falsity.

How could the aspirant receive such limitless generosity

from his guide,

such care and attention,

such nurturing and unconditional love,

if he were not worthy?

And it becomes clear to him

that the guide has never considered him unworthy.

His guide—who expresses so much more clarity

than the aspirant ever knew before,

so much more knowledge

than he ever thought possible

and so much more understanding and vision

than the aspirant had ever experienced—

has never considered him unworthy.

The guide has spent time and effort in relation to him—

certainly not because he considers the aspirant unworthy.

The guide always relates to him free of conditions,

always regards him with acceptance and respect

and has always given him unconditional love,

from the beginning.

The aspirant recognizes he is known without pretense.

> He is loved for himself,
>
> not for any fronts he might put up.
>
> This inspires him to drop his guard
>
> and with it his fear
>
> and the pressure of pretense.
>
> He learns the delight of relaxing,
>
> trusting in his Being
>
> and expressing his Being as he is, in the moment,
>
> expressing all the beautiful qualities of true Being:
>
> honesty, strength, faithfulness, perseverance,
>
> integrity, loyalty, love.
>
> He experiences a deeper knowledge of who he is.

Through the guide's—the royal Being's—devotion

> to the Being that the aspirant is,
>
> the aspirant learns devotion to Self.

Through devotion to the Being that *is*—through devotion to reality—

> the aspirant learns devotion to Self.

Through Devotion to the Being that you are—

through Devotion to Reality—

learn Devotion to Self.

Something in people often opposes this,

> the guide tells the aspirant.

> They have learned that it is fine to be devoted to someone else
> but not to Self.

> The hypocrisy of false modesty contradicts devotion to Self:

> false modesty is founded on

> the mistaken perception of isolation,

> which is rooted in relating to oneself as ego.

The Hypocrisy of false Modesty contradicts Devotion to Self:
false Modesty is founded on the mistaken Perception of Isolation,
which is rooted in relating to oneself as Ego.

The aspirant has learned to see Self as One:

> the power of Being that is the essence of every *form* of Being,

> just as the ocean is the essence of every wave.

The Power of Being is the Essence of every Form of Being,
just as the Ocean is the Essence of every Wave.

Individuals who fail to be devoted to Self

> neglect the relationship to their essence,

the essence of all,

the infinite.

The guide says to the aspirant,

Neglect of Self

establishes a strong sense of isolation from yourself.

This causes the faculties—

the aspects that are to relate to Self—

to disconnect from Being.

When your mind, feelings and emotions, for example,

are disconnected from the Being you are,

they do *not* relate to *you* their experiences

of the world around you and within you.

That is why you feel emptiness, lack and need.

Additionally, the real you is the source of the faculties' power.

When you choose isolation

and thereby disconnect your faculties from their source, Self,

they become disempowered.

Then you feel weak, unworthy

and all the symptoms that follow:

anxiety, depression, despair, hopelessness, fear, addiction...

As you know now,

devotion to Self is a fundamental necessity

for the successful relationship of your various aspects

to the Being that you are.

When your faculties were not integrated with you,

they were not *devoted* to Self,

you were not integrated with the whole.

Being a fully integrated individual is a fundamental necessity for successful relationship with all.

The initiate says frankly to her guide,

I am not accustomed to relating to myself with devotion,

and even though I now understand how important it is,

I often forget.

The guide smiles at her,

Devotion to Self needs to be permanent.

It is not a luxury.

It cannot be subject to moods or any other conditions.

Devotion is not something to indulge in from time to time,

when you have had a few nips of inspiration

or when you feel romantic, for example.

Devotion to Self

is not to be indulged in from Time to Time

during Moments of Inspiration

or romantic Feelings.

Devotion to Self has to be permanent.

Many fail to be devoted to Self.

The ultimate expression of lack of devotion to oneself is to say,

'I do not have time for this.'

The guide looks straight through the aspirant's eyes
into her soul,
Ask such a person, 'You do not have time for being you?'

Ask yourself now, have you taken the time to be consciously focused
on becoming expert at devotion to Self?

The guide continues,
When individuals are not devoted to Self,
is it any wonder that they experience frustration and failure,
that they do not have a successful relationship with themselves
or with others?

Many are frightened by the prospect
of *not* being distracted from themselves.
What *enmity* of Self!
That is like an organism allergic to itself.

And is that not the prevailing case?
How much time do most individuals spend
engaged with distractions?
How often do they cultivate the distraction
of anxiety, inner turmoil, even fear?
Those repetitive behaviors
are ways of escaping awareness of Self.
Why do you think these teachings are so challenging
to so many?

There are teachers who attract thousands of people,
as long as their teachings are less focused on Self.

They might provide some nice sensual experiences
or some psychologically soothing moments
that make individuals feel better temporarily.
But the temporary is soon forgotten
and does not add to real growth.

The guide indicates to the initiate to be very attentive:
Growth is what everyone wants, whether they realize it or not.
Without growth they will always suffer lack and need,
dysfunction and despair.
But the growth has to be *real* and deep-reaching,
not momentary and superficial.
It has to be lasting.
Growth has to be purposefully dedicated
to living true to one's real identity:
thinking, feeling and functioning permanently true to Self.
There is a strong resistance to that.
To overcome the resistance to real growth,
to the change toward Self,
is liberation.

> To overcome the Resistance
> to the Change toward Self
> is Liberation.

Recognize this, says the guide:
>people can feel validated in their involvement
>with the momentary and superficial,
>for it is of the realm of murk to which they are accustomed.
>Fellow members of the murky realm easily welcome anyone
>to join in their self-denying ways of being.
>And as you know by now,
>since ego runs the murky realm,
>most suffer from the illusion that they love it there.

The guide explains,
>Spiritual aspirants are often frightened
>at the prospect of being in touch with Self,
>living the Self we are.
>They have a habitual stance of opposition to Self.

Due to a history of allegiance to a false identity—ego—
>individuals have learned to fear the real Self they are.
>Fear fosters isolation.
>Isolation is a direct product of lack of devotion to Self.
>Devotion to Self fosters the experience of interconnectedness,
>wholeness of Being.

We are so wonderfully constructed
>that when we do not experience the fullness of Being,
>our signals tell us something is wrong,
>something is *lacking*.
>Since people are so industrious,
>they attempt to make up the lack

by accruing various objects, situations,
conditions, circumstances, powers.

When they have amassed enough objects,
they are seduced by the power inherent
in having so many objects
with which they can intimidate others
and appear to gain more prestige and power.
All the while, the more objects they accrue,
the more anxious and dissatisfied they feel.

What do they do then? asks the guide.
They try to accrue *more* objects that do not satisfy them.
What happens when they accrue more objects
that do not satisfy them?
Do they become more satisfied or more *dis*satisfied?
They become more dissatisfied.

Do people perform actions to be more dissatisfied? asks the guide.
No, certainly not.
However, people who are in illusion
regard the teachings of reality as illusion,
and illusion as reality;
they regard their pursuit of objects
that persistently yield dissatisfaction
as actually being for their satisfaction.
Their dissatisfaction is tangible.

> People who are in Illusion
> regard the Teachings of Reality as Illusion,
> and Illusion as Reality.

Remember, distraction and dissatisfaction
>   are techniques to avoid being yourself.
>   Although people experience great pleasure in these teachings,
>   when they are under the sway of illusion
>   it may still appear to them as if liberation were a prison,
>   as if joy were suffering.

> Remember,
> Distraction and Dissatisfaction are Techniques
> to avoid being yourself.

Somehow people's perceptions can turn topsy-turvy.
>   People were taught that it is frightening to be yourself,
>   and if they were ever to show themselves without fronts,
>   something very nasty would be revealed.
>   That is why they have attached themselves to the distractions
>   by which they avoid being real.

Let this sink in, says the guide with strong emphasis:
> when individuals keep returning to the dysfunctional behaviors
> rooted in ego,
> they harm themselves and those around them,
> maintaining an attachment to behaviors
> they may even know to be to their detriment.
> Their attachment to non-self is even more addictive
> than the attachment to alcohol is for some.

The Attachment to Non-self is the worst Addiction.

The guide lovingly says to the aspirant,
> Here is another fact you do well never to forget:
> everyone wants to be loved.
> Everyone wants to be loved.
> To receive love as the Being you really are
> and to give love
> is the deepest fulfillment.
> Yet so many do so many things,
> subtly and overtly,
> to ensure they are not loved.
> Why should love seem so frightening or painful?
> It absolutely is not.
> It is foolish to insist on behaving toward love
> with so much fear.

> Everyone wants to be loved.

Are you afraid of love? Really now.

The aspirant is deeply impressed
> by the elaborate designs the king himself has gone through
> to help her discover herself
> and pull away from her attachment
> to the realm of suffering—
> what love, what care, what valuing!

The queen has always given him unconditional acceptance,
> absolute love.
> Feeling totally accepted and loved by the highest,
> he is able to reciprocate and love the royal Being, the king,
> the queen herself,
> without reservation.
> He is filled with a pervasive experience of freedom
> and a deep feeling of agreement with himself.

This opens in him the floodgates
> to experiencing the full array of emotions and feelings,
> all the ways in which he perceives.
> He is able to experience on every level,
> with every fiber, every atom, every vibration.
> He is aware on levels of subtlety he never imagined possible.

Now the king's Being is not some abstract notion,

    not some principle or idea,

    not some strange outside power,

    but her very source.

She had lost contact,

    and it was her life goal to regain contact with her source.

    Being truly with the king fills our aspirant with great joy

    and a bliss beyond anything she ever experienced before.

    She delights in being open like a flower in full bloom.

And through the power of realization

    comes the most important discovery:

    through the queen's love for him, he is able to love the queen

    and, in turn, to unconditionally love himself.

    This is a profound transformation.

In the unconditional love for himself,

    he experiences limitlessness.

    This is the experience of infinitude.

    In removing all limitations from himself,

    he understands fully how the royal realm has no boundaries.

The guide points out to the initiate,

    The realm is filled with the king—it *is* the king;

    the king is everywhere

    all the time,

    infinite.

The queen is the infinite realm,
> and at the same time she is transcendent to all its parts
> and to all events therein.
> She is not limited,
> not contained,
> not bound by any facet thereof.

The aspirant feels he has not the words to fully describe it;
> he simply *knows* the quietly balanced bliss
> of being in the experience of complete devotion to,
> and absorption in, infinite Being.
> This is the *unitive state*,
> this is the real meaning of *yoga*.

She learns to love the infinite
> and to completely and forever overcome
> the greatest of all barriers in her path:
> feeling that she is unworthy,
> that she does not belong.

Do you regard yourself as worthy to belong in the royal realm?

She dwells now in the unitive state,
> and through this she fulfills herself joyously
> in the realm of love and devotion.
> She has grown in the deepest aspects
> and knows the most precious part of the royal realm.

The aspirant experiences a sense of limitless gratitude
> and deep joyous devotion to her guide,

to the king, the queen.

Even her ego wants to prostrate itself before the royal Being.

Our aspirant says deep within her heart:

Feel this along with the aspirant.

I love Thee

I thank Thee

I adore Thee

I am one with Thee

I am That

That Thou art

Limitless Being

Self

This is a powerful shift in him.

In the past, whenever he had said,

'I am,'

it had been a statement of the ego,

even when he knew better:

'I am this mind,'

'I am this isolated personality.'

But now, 'I am' means his illimitability,
the infinity of Being.

The aspirant is so filled with the joy of Being
that every part of him is now completely willing
to be absorbed in the experience.
There is no more holding back,
no more hesitancy.

In self-recognition, in this all-out *I-Amness*,
his ego, too, is freed from the falsity of limitation.
'I am' now simply means, I am,
free of the limiting adjuncts,
free of modification.
Being is it.

Ego no longer wants to struggle,
to compete, deceive, divide.
It no longer wants to project artificial images
that cause ignorance, illusion, confusion and pride.

She has no more need for distraction or dissipation.
The aspirant feels released from need.
She experiences the satisfaction of *desirelessness*;
there is no more than the infinitude of Being.

She is open to the full experience of the infinite power of Being:
she can feel that,
know that,
breathe that,

experience that,
be that.

Now her knowledge is limitless;
the aspirant's knowledge is the queen's knowledge,
the queen's knowledge is the aspirant's knowledge.

The aspirant's mind is no longer bound to sense and thought,
but it is the queen's mind, the king's mind,
the infinite mind.
There is but one mind.

His unitive mind reflects him to himself,
as do his feelings and emotions—
all his instruments of perception
reflect him to himself with unconditional acceptance.
He is fully at peace and in harmony with the Being he is.
He is on all levels filled with love.

> Love is the Experience and Expression
> of Interconnectedness realized.

The aspirant has fully absorbed now the greatest of all power,
love and devotion.
She says to her guide,
This is it. Finally I am here.

The initiate is excited
    and feels truly prepared to finally enter
    the court of the king's realm.
    He stands back, waiting for the fanfare and the light show,
    the celestial maidens to come dancing forth—
    there is still a remnant in him
    that is waiting for the holy miracle
    and all the cheap thrills that come along with it.
    It is amazing what we allow conditioning to do.

And the guide says unto the aspirant,
    Good—so far. There is just a bit further to go...

THE INNER COURT

The guide speaks lovingly to the aspirant:

And you could include yourself in this experience.

Let us be together here now
> in a state of deep relaxation.
> Let every facet of you be radiant
> with the experience of limitless interconnected Self—
> every cell, every atom, every vibration
> be imbued with love.

Allow yourself to experience
> the unhindered flow of the king's essential force,
> the source of your vitality,
> your power to be.

Feel yourself as this vibrant essence,
> experience and know yourself as infinite Being
> expressed through your mind, body and senses,
> through all aspects of you.

With loving care prepare yourself
> so your conscious experience will be continuous and lasting
> as you proceed on your journey through eternity.

Be deeply at peace,

> connected with the king's appointed guide,
>
> at home in the royal realm.

Experience the joy, comfort, beauty

> and the deep security
>
> of the royal realm of Being in which you dwell.
>
> This is so satisfying it is worth your full focus.

The guide sits with the aspirant as they share in experience.

> He acknowledges the great advancement
>
> the initiate has accomplished:
>
> You have learned to enjoy the steps you have taken
>
> through the four gates.
>
> And you know now that with each step
>
> you have actually been in the realm of the king.

You have completed your lessons faithfully

> and resolved many struggles successfully.
>
> This has honed your faculties,
>
> strengthened and fine-tuned them
>
> and empowered you to progress more deeply and subtly
>
> toward the core of the queen's realm.

Through experience

> your understanding has become brilliant and clear.
>
> You have recognized real Self,
>
> opening to the deepest knowledge within you.

You have become privileged to the secret teachings
>of how the king thinks, feels, acts, lives—*is*.
>They are secret because they are unknown to most.
>For many generations these teachings were only imparted
>to students who had undergone rigorous disciplines,
>demonstrated sincerity and devotion
>and could transfer the teachings by word-of-mouth.
>Few have had the privilege and opportunity
>of exposure to what you have so richly received.

The guide continues in acknowledgement:
>You have learned to overcome the persistent seduction
>of familiar patterns that bind you to misery and pain.

You have learned that you can claim your place in the royal realm
>by simply and sincerely
>*living* in the knowledge you have gained:
>living as the queen lives,
>feeling as the king feels,
>seeing, hearing, speaking, relating, working and playing
>as the royal Being does.

You have learned to act in the recognition
>that you are not this little body-mind complex,
>but the limitless eternal self-knowing Being.
>This has inspired and empowered you
>to let go of your attachment to ego's deceptions
>and to act in harmony with what is, with reality,
>to act with success and the deepest joy,

fulfilling the real you,

not attempting to appease someone you are not.

You are expertly applying your sincere will

to practice your ability to respond—

your *responsibility*.

Responsibility is the ability to respond.

Without it you are as dull and unresponsive

as an impaired person.

In the exercise of responsibility

you can find great joy and empowerment.

You gain freedom and experience interconnectedness.

> Responsibility is the Ability to respond.

Now you are clear about your identity, the guide continues,

thus everything within you

sings with the joy of love and devotion to Self.

You know that all is integral to the king;

thus you need not fear.

The king stands balanced in complete tranquility

with one foot upon the dwarf of ignorance and illusion

amidst all the wild changes of nature,

the processes of creation and destruction.

He prevails steadily through the fires of evolution
with his hand lifted gently, saying,
'Fear not, you are limitless all-pervasive power of Being.'
He is unmoving Being tranquil in his whirling dance.

You are the steady strength of the power of Being that is infinite.
Even your ego and its resistances need not be feared;
they are part of the play.
Illusion, false perceptions, ego are but veils,
apparent negations of what really is.

What do the negations claim?
That you are not power,
that you are not conscious,
that you are not being,
and that you are not the power of Being:
that you *are* not.

The negations are merely figments of a distracted and distorted mind.
So you need not fear.
As you assert your essential Beingness,
the negations and fear cease,
for you cease giving power to ego's falsity.

As you joyously dedicate all your actions, feelings and thoughts
to the Being that you really are,
you are freed from the appearance of lack and need,
loneliness, fear, deprivation—
all the symptoms of the illusion of non-being.

The guide states lovingly,

> You see, the king has created *all*,
> including the realm of illusion and falsity,
> with the *implicit covenant* that we have everything we need—
> all the ability, all the faculties, all the potential—
> to find our way back to reality,
> which is our source.
> However, some do not trust in the reality of Being,
> thus they wallow in suffering.

The human life path is to *realize* our highest potential:

> to experience and continuously live
> according to our real identity,
> the essential power of Being.
> That is the fulfillment of evolution.
> There is a point where you have to make a conscious choice
> for Self-realization,
> a full commitment to the Self you are,
> with absolute self-acceptance.
> This is the stance of all-embracing real love.

The human Life Path is to *realize* our highest Potential:
to experience and continuously live
according to our real Identity,
the essential Power of Being.
That is the Fulfillment of Evolution.
There is a Point where you have to make a conscious Choice
for Self-realization,
a full Commitment to the Self you are,
with absolute Self-acceptance.
This is the Stance of all-embracing real Love.

The earthly love affairs are but dry runs for this real love.
The consummation of the ultimate love affair
is merging all your faculties in absolute devotion
with infinite Being:
your mind thinks and asserts for you,
'I am infinite Being';
your feelings feel and your senses sense,
'I am infinite Being';
everything about you experiences and expresses,
'I am infinite Being.'
That is the state of love that lastingly fulfills you.
All-pervasive Being is your true lover, your eternal lover,
the source of all love.

That lover is never fickle, always reliable,
and will never leave you.

It dawns on the aspirant
>that she never had been in a *meaningful* relationship
>until she met her guide.
>She asks, How do I conduct a relationship that includes
>acceptance and love
>and all the other elements that make it work?

The guide, pleased by the question, replies,
>Relationship includes, even on the mundane level,
>a commitment.
>How would it be if you said to your lover,
>'If you want to love me and be loved by me, go ahead'?
>It does not work that way;
>there must be a merging of not only body and mind,
>emotions, feelings and intellect,
>but—most importantly—
>intimate identity experienced in interconnectedness.
>This is what the king is offering you.

> Successful Relationship
> requires not only the Merging of Body and Mind,
> Emotions, Feelings and Intellect,
> but—most importantly—
> intimate Identity experienced in Interconnectedness.

That you will consciously step into the reality of Being
> with your full agreement and will
> is inevitable—
> even if it takes eons of time
> and enormous suffering
> before you consciously and proactively take that step.

The covenant is that you *can* do it and you *will*;
> *when* is up to you.

So now, the guide says to the aspirant,
> we are almost there
> but for one more thing,
> and it is a big one.

What good is it to have knowledge of the king, the queen
> and their realm,
> to master the science of the soul,
> to be accomplished in egoless service,
> to be able to love all, including even yourself,

unless your life is a *constant enactment* of the reality of you,
a testament to who and what you are?

Do you think you can live in the royal realm
and still have the option to go on vacation
in the realm of murk?
Who wants that?
The habitual false identity, ego.
Ego pretends it is hard work to live in the realm of fulfillment.

Imagine this:
you are invited by the queen
into the inner court of the royal realm,
and they bathe and anoint you,
dress you in fresh white linen
and have you eating at the queen's table laden with ambrosia,
but every once in a while you go off
to roll around in the murky gutter
with the slime and fleas,
as your vacation—
'This visit to the royal realm is great,
but I need to go home, forget it for a while
and have a good time'—
as if wallowing in suffering were a good time!

The ego wants to treat you like a fish on a hook.
When a deep-sea fisherman pursuing big game hooks a fish,
what does the fish do?
He jumps and flies with all speed toward liberation.

What does the skillful fisherman do, jerk back?

No, he gives him some line, lets him run.

This tires the fish.

And then the fisherman reels him in.

Your old patterns are the hook

by which ego pulls you back into bondage.

Through your old patterns ego lets you think

that every once in a while you can go straight toward liberation

without doing anything real about it:

the illusion of entitlement

without responsibility and contribution.

The moment ego sees you are not alert anymore,

you are not vigilant, expert and loving,

ego employs the patterns to reel you in again.

That is why you need to be an *Expert In Life*.

Always remember this, says the guide with serious meaning:

leading your life according to its real purpose is not a hobby,

it is not a game to play as the mood strikes you;

it requires that you keep your faculties in integrity,

in a continuously loyal love relationship with the reality

of who you are.

Leading your Life according to its real Purpose is not a Hobby,
it is not a Game to play as the Mood strikes you.
It requires that you keep your Faculties in Integrity,
in a continuously loyal Love Relationship with the Reality of
who you are.

Your personal integrity has profound significance.

> You need to be able to depend on your determination:
> when you say you will do something, it will be done.

Loyalty is also important.

> Respond loyally and sensibly to what you have learned.

The aspirant feels the need to have a deeper understanding

> of the important points her guide is revealing.
> She appeals to him,
> Please help me experience conducting life
> true to Being that I am.

You need to direct your actions

> according to the knowledge you have gained.
> Cease acting according to the previous ignorance
> or misconceptions.
> How many times
> do you need to be hit over the head with a hammer

to get the message that it is painful
and not advantageous to you?

> Learn from your learning Experiences.

Will I then finally succeed? asks the aspirant.

The guide replies,

> To arrive at your goal,
> you need to function in accord with what you know
> regarding the reality of who you are.
> If you do not live the Being that you are in constancy,
> your involvement with the reality of Self is momentary.
> Self is real, the momentary is not.
> With the unreal you contradict Self,
> and disappointment is sure to follow.
> To be real, but not with constancy, is a self-contradiction.
> Unless you *enact* the Being that you are constantly,
> you will not be in the realm of reality.

> *Enact* the Being that you are, constantly,
> and you will be in the Realm of Reality.

You do not become a permanent member of the realm
        and make the realm your home
        by just doing egoless service
        or good practice
        or good deeds.
        It is by truly and constantly living as the king lives.

That seems so difficult, the aspirant says.

The guide responds,
        What is difficult is repeatedly creating the illusory life
        through attachment to old patterns seated in the past
        by which you cut your own throat.

I have tried and I have failed, says the aspirant,
        because my old patterns sabotage me again and again.

Listen carefully, says the guide,
        and I will tell you how to succeed:
        free yourself once and for all from your dysfunctional patterns.
        You accomplish this by permanently engaging in all actions
        as the self-knowing power of Being you are
        and thereby give up acting as ego with the old patterns
        that you say sabotage you again and again.

You have to change the way you relate to yourself,
        the way you relate to objects, people, time and space—
        everything:
        you are Being,
        all that *is* is Being.

Being is the connective substance that is the foundation
of the union of all that is.

To succeed,
free yourself once and for all from your dysfunctional Patterns.
Permanently engage in all Actions
as the self-knowing Power of Being you are
and thereby give up acting as Ego
with the old Patterns that sabotage you.
Change the Way you relate to yourself,
the Way you relate to Objects, People, Time and Space—
everything:
you are Being,
all that *is* is Being.
Being is the connective Substance that is the Foundation
of the Union of all that is.

Everything has to be in a clear, continuous, loyal relationship
with reality,
with the Self that you are.
If you do not recognize the grass you sit on
as yet another manifestation of royal Being,
you are missing something.
If you do not recognize that the birds above or the bugs below

are of the same royal essence,
you are still disconnected.
Every sound you hear
is the song of the queen in self-expression.

Imagine if, for the entertainment of your limited senses,
the limitless queen appeared before you and spoke to you—
of love, of wisdom, of guidance—
would you just stand there picking your nose
and look away in distraction
or even drift off and go to sleep?
Would you not be completely present?
If the love of your life appeared for a moment,
would you not be entirely present?

Eternal Being is right here with you every moment,
right in front of you
and next to you
and behind you
and right within you.

The power of Being is all about you, right now,
revealing Self to you
through every blade of grass,
through the humming of every bee
and the flight of every bird,
through anything and everything.

> Infinite Being is speaking *to* you
> and *through* you
> all the Time.

Yes, says the aspirant,

> I do want to know and experience infinite Being.
> Please help me further to understand how I can.

The guide says,

> There is a common refrain throughout humanity:
> 'If only infinite Being were to reveal himself to me
> then I could believe in him:
> Self, please just give me a sign.'
> But look around:
> there is constant proof of infinite Being's presence.
> Does he have to hit you over the head with a hammer
> and shout, 'That was me!'?

Limitless Being is right here.

> You are limitless Being.
> Infinite Being is in your heart.
> Can you get any closer than that?
> There is no distance nor secret from infinite Being,
> for Being is sheer power,
> indivisible, all-pervasive, limitless *One*.

Are we as human beings, on a practical level,

     capable of experiencing infinite Being's presence?

     Are we capable of the *awareness* of Being?

We know Being is not an object,

     but pure force,

     limitless, all-pervasive and eternal,

     the essence of all that is.

The guide asks,

     Are you capable of experiencing Being while you are alive?

     Of course you are, it is the most important reason for this life.

     What good would your life be

     if you could not experience it,

     if you could not experience yourself as Being?

     What good is your life

     when you are not experiencing yourself in it?

     Many people have the opinion

     that after death we are united with infinite Being.

     This does not make sense.

> What good would your Life be
> if you could not experience it,
> if you could not experience yourself as Being?
> What good is your Life
> when you are not experiencing yourself in it?

You must remember, says the guide,

> what I have helped you experience
> regarding the union of you and royal Being.
> You must have the conscious willingness
> to experience that oneness,
> that love relationship,
> as the foundation of all your experience of Being.
> Infinite Being does not need this,
> *you* need it, if you want to experience yourself in reality:
> *that* you are and as *who* you are.

You can also volunteer to experience separateness and suffering.

> As you have learned, in the infinite there is no need.
> Certainly there is no need in the infinite for us to do anything.
> However, when we behave as if separate,
> we are misrepresenting the Being that we are.
> Do you want to misrepresent yourself?

No, says the aspirant fervently,

> I no longer want to deny or misrepresent
> infinite interconnected Being.
> I know that to be my true identity.
> But, please tell me,
> how do I recognize the experience of being infinite Being?

The guide tenderly smiles at her,

> When your inner lover, your inner voice speaks,
> do you know it as limitless Being's voice,
> the voice of your real identity?

And do your faculties respond in unity,

loyally and lovingly?

Then you are certain of your experience of infinite Being.

There may be times, says the guide, when something in you says,

'That is the voice of authority, I have to go against it.'

Most individuals have grown up with an authority issue.

In the insensitive realm of murk they had to protect themselves

from the intrusion of imposed authority.

When your faculties oppose your inner voice—

your own authority—

you are in conflict and confusion,

behaving in ways that hurt you

and distract you from the bliss and joy

inherent to the infinite Being you are.

Then you are fighting against the *real* authority,

you are fighting against truth, love and interconnectedness,

you are fighting against yourself.

When you hear the voice of Self,

you are listening to the voice of real authority,

the voice within:

the author of your life.

> The Voice of Self
> is the Voice of real Authority,
> the Voice within:
> the Author of your Life.

The strength of the inner lover, the Inner Knower,
>   is your source of infinite empowerment;
>   it is the ultimate authority.
>   The Inner Knower knows reality, without mistake or doubt.
>   Do you relate to limitless Being's voice as your voice?
>   Do you know it as the voice of your real identity?

Do you relate to limitless Being's voice as your voice?

The guide asks the initiate,
>   Have you ever listened to the voice of knowledge within you
>   and *not* responded to it?
>   Then you know the price you pay without fail.

Have you ever listened to the voice of the Inner Knower
>   and *responded* to it?
>   Then you know how clear, clean and together that feels within.
>   Even more wonderful does it feel
>   when you live according to your inner voice constantly
>   and do not wait for its pronouncements.

The way you have learned to relate to me, says the guide,

    has helped you to know how to relate loyally, lovingly

    and with constancy to yourself.

> Your Relationship with the Guide
>
> is the primary Example
>
> that stimulates your subtler Relationship
>
> with the Inner Knower.

The aspirant's devotion to the royal Being, to the king-queen-guide,

    has now grown so strong and steady

    that he responds to all his guide's teachings

    by placing himself into their *conscious experience*

    immediately and permanently—really.

    When you love,

    are you not willing to do anything for that person?

    That is how the aspirant feels toward the luminous Self

    who functions as guide.

His guide imparts the teachings of the sages

    regarding the relationship to the guide:

Who is the Guide?
The Guide is royal Being
in the Awareness of his All-pervasiveness
with which he guides those Aspects of himself
who are in the Illusion of Separateness
toward the Realization of their Interconnectedness.

The aspirant is deeply impressed and inspired
      by her guide's description.
      She wants to know,
      Then what am I?

Who is the Aspirant?
The Aspirant is royal Being in the Guise of Separateness
who is being guided by infinite Being
into the Experience of Interconnectedness.

Knowing how important this is, the initiate petitions the guide,
      Please lead me through the experience
      by which I will have real understanding of
      how to relate to you, my guide, effectively.

Please focus deeply, says the guide,
>   so you experience fully the following teachings,
>   as they are of cardinal importance to you
>   in your workings with your guide,
>   as well as with yourself and your life.

There are three types of relationship to the guide:

The middling relationship
>   is to listen to what the guide says and respond by doing it.

The lesser relationship to the guide
>   is to listen to what the guide says and not respond to it.

The highest relationship
>   is to anticipate what the guide will say
>   and do it before the guide has a chance to verbalize it;
>   then the consciousness of the guide
>   and the consciousness you are,
>   are realized as one.
>   This is meaningful to you only
>   when you realize the Being you are is the Being the guide is.
>   The Being you are is the Being the guide is.

There are three Types of Relationship to the Guide:

The *middling* Relationship
is to listen to what the Guide says
and respond by doing it.

The *lesser* Relationship
is to listen to what the Guide says
and not respond.

The *highest* Relationship
is to anticipate what the Guide will say
and do it before the Guide has a Chance to verbalize it;
then the Consciousness of the Guide
and the Consciousness you are
are one.
This is meaningful to you only
when you realize the Being you are is the Being the Guide is.

All you have to do is live as the Being you are.
Respond to the Inner Knower
and the guide does not have to say much any more.
You just are being Being together.

Our aspirant has no loyalty left to non-being.
She states with clarity,

It does not make sense
to act in ways that are ignorant and self-injuring.
She is so loyal to Being that she is now free
from the twisted manipulations of the realm of murk.
The pain and suffering of being in the land of murk
no longer have the power to fool her,
no longer attract or mislead her.
Through self-loyalty she removes the obstacles within herself.
The invasive patterns have no more power over her,
for she has taken charge.

The aspirant has no tolerance for negative patterns of behavior;
she will not invite them in,
she will not let them fester and suck out all her energy
and return her to pain and sorrow.
She will not give them an opportunity.

> When you do not give Energy to your internal Obstacles
> they have no Power to waylay you.

The aspirant takes energy away from the negative
by placing his energy into the positive.
He has enough intelligence, self-respect and self-love
to instantly and permanently

enact all the knowledge of the queen's realm
as he gains it.

The guide tests him further,
    Imagine there were two types of food:
    one that is poisoned and comes from the realm of murk,
    and one food that is life-sustaining
    and comes from the king's realm.
    In ignorance you might eat either one.
    Now the guide says to you,
    'If you partake of that food
    you will have a painful death of poisoning.
    If you eat this food
    you will have health, power and beauty for eternity.'
    How long a learning process would you allow yourself
    to respond according to your guide's teaching?
    Would you allow any possibility to exist
    of eating the poison?

Are you not capable of responding that decisively,
    that permanently and predictably,
    to the knowledge of Self you have gained?

Do you understand what this does to your evolutionary process?
    says her guide.
    You make quantum leaps in your evolution.
    Evolution, which has taken eons and eons of time
    to get you to this point,

you can complete in this lifetime
with your conscious knowing participation.

With joy streaming from his eyes,
  the guide acknowledges the aspirant:
  You have grown into a sincerely willing and expert student,
  an expert at learning,
  an expert at being.
  Your progress has become easy, quick,
  powerful, lasting and joyous.
  Remember this:
  when you remove loyalty from who you are *not*
  by placing your loyalty upon who you *are,*
  your progress is no longer challenging or frightening
  or laborious,
  your progress is enjoyable.

When you remove Loyalty from who you are *not*
by placing your Loyalty upon who you *are,*
your Progress is no longer challenging or frightening
or laborious,
your Progress is enjoyable.

The guide cautions the aspirant,
  If your learning and practice seem like a chore,

it is the ego, not the Self that is functioning.
Your attention is then not with yourself;
you are distracted.

Our aspirant commits himself to his essence,
to everything integral to him,
with deep devotion.
He commits himself to dwelling in clarity
in the joy of interconnectedness
without breaks.

He determines to live congruent to his Being
sincerely, continuously, expertly, without backsliding
and with trust in the Being that he is.
And, most importantly,
he backs up this powerful determination
by immediately initiating true action
that will always be followed *absolutely*—
free of variance, forgetfulness and complication—
by actions true to this vow!

He recognizes this is not difficult.
Difficulty only occurs when he gives the patterns of opposition
the energy to revitalize;
then they become re-established through repetition.

If you were in a poisoned atmosphere, says the guide,
and found a safety house,

you would not leave the door open
to let the poison come in with you.

Now the aspirant understands the reason for the four gates.
She understands the gift of the guide's first challenge:
'Are you qualified?'
It was not a question of being judged,
as he remembers he felt;
it was a matter of immediate, as well as ultimate, practicality.
You have to prepare yourself and be ready
to become an Expert In Life.
She has become more finely attuned, perceptive
and trusting of herself.

The guide emphasizes,
Each of the four gates expands your perception
to limitlessness.
The gates are there, not to keep you out,
but to empower you truly
to come into the very core of the queen's realm,
to recognize with understanding and vision
and *realize* your true Self:
to Self-realize.

When you went through the gate of knowledge,
you learned that knowledge is the most direct means
to enter the realm of fulfillment.
Without real knowledge about yourself
you cannot direct your faculties,

you cannot inspire yourself.

You cannot *be* yourself without knowing who you are.

Thus, honor your knowledge of Being.

Without real Knowledge about yourself

you cannot direct your Faculties,

you cannot inspire yourself.

You cannot *be* yourself without knowing who you are.

Thus, honor your Knowledge of Being.

The guide continues,

> When you went through the gate of the science of Self,
> you recognized that abstaining from behaviors contrary to Self
> and cultivating behaviors congruent to Self—
> harmlessness, non-grasping, positive observances
> and meditation—
> are the most direct means
> for attaining the core of the king's realm.
> You became an expert at the science of Self.

Abstaining from Behaviors contrary to Self
and cultivating Behaviors congruent to Self—
Harmlessness, Non-grasping, positive Observances
and Meditation—
are the most direct Means
for attaining the Core of the King's Realm.

When you went through the gate of the meditation of action
        you learned to do action
        in effortlessly balanced consciousness—
        in meditation.
        You learned to act as the king acts.
        Thus you experienced the unitive state in action
        and found that to be the most direct means to the royal realm.
        In the unitive state you know you are Being
        who is manifesting—expressing Self—
        through everything and everyone and yourself.

> Do Action in effortlessly balanced Consciousness—
> in Meditation.
> Act as the King acts.
> Thus you experience the unitive State in Action,
> the most direct Means to the royal Realm.

The guide reminds her,

> When you went through the gate of love and devotion,
> you discovered love and devotion to be the most direct means
> of gaining the king's realm.
> You became a great devotee.

> Love and Devotion are the most direct Means
> of gaining the King's Realm.
> Become a great Devotee.

Each of the four gates is the most direct means—
> and each gate is indispensable—
> to entering the realm of eternal Being.

Be aware, says the guide,
> knowledge alone can be dry and empty,

distant and cold,

a plaything that the ego uses

to create confusion and rationalization.

Devotion without knowledge can be dangerous,

as detrimental as the blind urgings of nature:

without control, without direction

and just as greedy and unrefined.

Look at the wars.

The dark realm seems devoted

to destruction of its people and environment

because they lack knowledge—

not material knowledge,

not technical knowledge,

but knowledge of reality.

Even knowledge, devotion and love are not enough,

for they must be related to the moral, ethical

and practical expertise

learned in the science of Self.

Knowledge, devotion, love and the science of Self are not enough,

for they can be ephemeral and passing, not substantial;

they are momentary and without aim

if they are not *enacted* with the meditation of action.

If you do not act as royal Being acts,

then knowledge, love and expertise are merely superficial;

you will become disappointed and discouraged again.

Then you say, 'Nothing works. It is all hopeless.'

This makes for deeper depression.

And that is the ultimate hypocrisy.

Be aware:

Knowledge alone can be dry and empty, distant and cold,
a plaything of the ego to confuse and rationalize.

Devotion without Knowledge can be dangerous,
as detrimental as the blind Urgings of Nature:
without Control, without Direction
and just as greedy and unrefined.

Even Knowledge, Devotion and Love
are not enough,
for they must be related to the moral, ethical
and practical Expertise learned in the Science of Self.

Knowledge, Devotion, Love and the Science of Self
are not enough,
for they can be ephemeral and passing, not substantial;
they are momentary and without Aim
if they are not enacted with the Meditation of Action.

If you do not act as royal Being acts,
then Knowledge, Love and Expertise are merely superficial;
you will become disappointed and discouraged again.
Consequently you say, Nothing works. It is all hopeless.
This makes for deeper Depression.
And that is the ultimate Hypocrisy.

The guide suggests,

> You can make a scientific experiment
> with all you have learned.
> Sincerely implement through your own practice
> all the lessons you have gained traversing the four gates,
> and you will know clearly through your own experience,
> not from what I have told you
> and not from what someone else says,
> that reality works.
> *Reality works!*

Now that the aspirant has fully integrated

> the lessons of the four gates,
> she is able to proceed joyously, without hindrance or hesitation
> into the realm of the limitless Self,
> to enter the inner court,
> the very core of the kingdom of fulfillment and joy.

You, as well, may prepare yourself for this magnificent event,
> *as the guide prepares our aspirant.*

Her guide lovingly faces her again,

> Are you ready?
> Let your focus be pure and simple,
> deep in your center.
> Allow yourself to experience the joy
> as you enter the innermost court
> of the kingdom of fulfillment and bliss.

As the aspirant enters the inner court,

>
all the inhabitants welcome him with unconditional acceptance.
>
They greet him with open arms
>
and with the love of life-long recognition.

Open yourself to this experience now.

The aspirant recognizes the king in every member of the realm,

>
the queen in all her guises,
>
in all her self-expressions.

And through all of them

>
royal Being embraces the aspirant again and again,
>
revealing Self by different names:
>
Serenity, Grace, Harmony, Compassion,
>
Determination, Interconnectedness, Faith,
>
Clarity, Awareness, Integrity, Trust, Balance, Joy...

All the citizens of the royal realm

>
know all and recognize all;
>
all live as one.

There is a constant healing, loving, nurturing, illumining energy

>
emanating from them all.
>
This energy is their very spirit,
>
their essence,
>
their Being—
>
your spirit, your essence, your Being.

The guide warmly shares with the aspirant:

> Feel the healing, loving, illumining energy
>
> emanating from your core to all,
>
> and let your core receive the same from all around you,
>
> nurturing you,
>
> embracing and including you.

You can allow yourself to feel this.

Experience the subtle energy now,

> the pure, joyous vibration of self-knowing Being.
>
> This is the family of real Self,
>
> the realm of Self,
>
> the king is Self, the queen is Self.
>
> Feel Self coursing through every fiber of you.
>
> You are Self.
>
> All are singing the wonderful symphony of Self.
>
> This is the all-pervasive infinite royal Self.

The aspirant is now utterly safe and secure.

Feel that in you.

There is no more appearance of boundaries;

> there are no limits.

The initiate *knows* herself in limitless expansiveness.

> She knows Self more fully and in finer detail
>
> than anything she might have considered possible,
>
> even in her wildest imaginations.

She discovers with the certainty of clarity
>that she is at home now.

Experience that absolute certainty.
>*Feel yourself as the aspirant, at home.*
>*You are home.*

The royal realm is where you came from;
>*this is where you were engendered.*

The initiate says to herself,
>I have returned home at last.
>I am home now.
>I am home.
>I am.

Her guide acknowledges,
>This is a profound realization.
>By a seeming accident of nature
>you were abducted and orphaned
>and ended up in the realm of murk.

You were challenged
>to bring yourself back to the realm of your heritage,
>the realm of light and joy,
>the realm of eternity,
>the realm where you know the fullness of Being.

You now know the royal realm is your birthright;
>you have finally returned to your original home.

Upon your path of return you have become expert
at living in all phases of infinite Being that you are.

The guide continues,

With all your facets you live in beautiful balance,
in clarity and completeness,
free, whole and fulfilled.

In this realm—your home—

you live love without conditions, without limit.
You love all,
and you no longer exclude yourself,
for, as you have learned to see the king
in all members of the realm,
you see yourself in all.

You see yourself as the king looking at himself.

You know yourself as the queen knowing herself.

Every Action expresses the limitless and intimate Unity
to which you know yourself to be integral.
From Moment to Moment,
Breath by Breath,
know yourself and experience yourself
to be the one royal Being.

The guide beams with joy:
> With abiding pleasure and infinite bliss
> take your place in the royal court.
> Your travels are complete.
> Rest in effortless balance and luminous joy.

And the guide invites the aspirant
> to enjoy looking back upon his travels:
> Having been of the royal realm eternally,
> you have always been Being.
> But you projected your consciousness into a *limited* state,
> into the *forgetfulness* of Being.
> There you experienced an illusory existence—
> gray, arid, painful and murky.
> You experienced the suffering of separateness and fear
> and the need to overcome isolation.
> You felt driven to return to your source.

This brought you to the outer gate of the king's realm
> where you met the guide
> who helped you traverse the evolutionary steps
> to knowing yourself in reality.

Again and again you recognized and asserted
> the power, beauty, luminosity and illimitability of Being
> that you are.
> As a manifestation of limitless Being,
> you have recognized and nurtured yourself
> as the power of Being we call the king, the queen.

Thus you know yourself in our wholeness,
in the oneness that we all are.

Now, as you look back at the realm of murk,
you recognize that it is only a chamber in the king's realm
caused by your own alchemy of illusion.

From your clear perception
you can see the inhabitants in the realm of murk
as aspects of all-pervasive Being
feeling left behind,
still attached to suffering
or wandering somewhere
on their path toward the king's realm.

You can assess them realistically
and recognize what they need to cease suffering
and be brought home,
for you are the royal Being who can fling open the gates.

Now you can welcome them to the realm of eternal fulfillment
and help guide them as you were guided.

The essence that you are is limitless, all-pervasive,
the same essence that all is.
You are the limitless Being
that is the essence and identity of all.

You can also recognize all the parts of your Being
that are at home now.

Cause everything within and about you to feel clear and strong,
aligned with the Being that you are.
Be Self in full consciousness.
Bring in any facets that may still be left behind,
all the way into the core of the queen's realm.
Do this now and maintain it always.
Feel yourself in the unitive state, whole.

The guide speaks with calm enthusiasm,
Dwell in clarity and self-awareness,
aware that you are aware of being aware,
knowing the Being that you are,
the luminous power of Being that is limitless,
all-pervasive and everlasting.

You are that.
Know that,
live that in vitality, fullness and joy—
permanently.

You are limitless all-pervasive Being,
dwelling in the joy of self-knowledge
in all the glorious beauty of the royal realm.
You are at peace, at home eternally.

The guide gives a strong instruction,
Cultivate a continuous attitude
by which you say within yourself,
'I am Being.

I am what has always been and shall always be.
I am aware of myself being aware,
knowing myself to be limitless in time and space.
Limitless in time
because I have always been
and shall always be—eternal Being.
Limitless in space
because I am all-pervasive Being,
everywhere all the time.'

Say within yourself,
I am Being.
I am what has always been and shall always be.
I am aware of myself being aware,
knowing myself to be limitless in Time and Space.
Limitless in Time
because I have always been
and shall always be—eternal Being.
Limitless in Space
because I am all-pervasive Being,
everywhere all the Time.

The aspirant is uplifted with inspiration and proclaims joyously,
This is profound realization!

I am time.

I am space.

I am that which is in all,

yet independent and transcendent to all,

for nothing can contain me,

infinite Being that I am.

I am purely that I am,

I am that.

The guide beams joyous love toward the initiate,

You will always be in full consciousness

when you keep the following awareness:

> I am Self.
>
> Self is the Essence of my Being.
>
> Self is the Essence of all Being.
>
> All are Manifestation of Self.
>
> There is but one Self, and that is limitless.
>
> I am Self.
>
> I act in Expression of Self I am.

May all have sufficient love for themselves

to enter through the four gates

and reach the core of the royal realm

in full Self-realization
in this lifetime.

I salute the power of Being that you are
and bow down ego before that.

The End
that is The Beginning.

Be in the Joy of Being

GLOSSARY OF TERMS

absolute: total, unqualified, undiminished; not subject to any limitation; existing independently.

animating energy: the creative force that gives life to creatures.

aspirant: spiritual student.

attachment: bond with the unreal, the momentary, illusion.

austerities: practices, disciplines, restraints.

authority issue: internal conflict and confusion regarding your own authority over your life.

avaricious: greedy for wealth, conditions or material gain.

being: the being that Being does; existing; manifesting Being.

Being: all that is being; the essential, all-pervasive, enduring, unitive power by which everything is; the irreducible identity of all life forms.

Beingness: term used to emphasize Being, the identity, over being, the act.

bliss: transcendent joy integral to the clear, undistracted and continuous experience of Being.

body-mind [construct, complex]: the combination of body, mind, emotions, feelings, intellect and intuition.

cause and effect: the law of nature relating all actions inexorably with their consequences.

cave of the heart: the area that the breath goes to, the general area of your heart; your center.

center: a chosen focal point in meditation, the area of your heart, which is limitless, free of boundaries; where you experience the awareness of Being, the light of consciousness.

circumstances and conditions: the momentary, ephemeral, the impermanent; the opposite of the permanence of essence.

commitment: aligning yourself with a specific choice and assuming responsibility for integrating it into your existence by living it.

concentration: the gathering of your energies (mental, emotional, intellectual, intuitional, physical and sensual) and fixing them at will upon a chosen point.

conditioning: patterns of reaction and behavior established through repetition.

conscious experience: being aware of Self purely, or in relation with objects and events (physical, sensual, emotional, mental, intellectual or intuitional).

conscious action: action in the awareness of Being; action in the experience and expression of yourself as totally interconnected, eternal, all-pervasive, conscious Being.

consciousness: the awareness or experience of Being.

core: your center of Being.

darkness: the absence of the light of self-awareness.

death: when a manifestation of Being ends and changes into another state of being.

denial: refusal to acknowledge reality.

depression: a dysfunctional state resulting from the repression of feeling and disregard of self-experience.

desirelessness: release from need; recognition that there is no more than the infinitude of Being.

destiny: the course of life molded by what you come into this life with and the conditioning and habits established in this life, as well as your determined actions.

devotee: one who lives in love and devotion to the reality of Self as the most direct means of gaining Self-realization.

direct experience: your experience, as opposed to belief or hearsay.

distraction: mind's meandering in thoughts unrelated to the moment of being, that tend to enmesh mind in matters that cause you to suffer in dysfunction, deprivation and disappointment.

dysfunction: self-opposing behaviors resulting from being out of touch with your real Self; a block to the inherent tendency to flourish.

ego: the false perception of identity as an isolated body-mind-emotions-feelings-intellect-intuition construct.

ego-actions: attitudes and actions based upon the perception of yourself as an isolated and limited entity, such as, dishonesty, greed and pride.

ego-doership: false perception of a limited isolated entity acting.

emotion: an expressive state; a subtle, internal response to an experience.

emptiness: an undesirable state where your faculties are disconnected from the Being you are and do not relate to you their experiences of the world around you and within you.

empty: opposite of full or fulfilled.

equanimity: balance; evenness of mind.

essence: that which makes you what you are; the absolute, irreducible substance of you; that which upholds everything about you; your unchanging identity; that without which you could not be.

evolution: growth toward the highest state; integration with the whole; continuous process of development toward a state free of limitation; the process by which the manifestations of Being grow toward recognition of themselves as the one limitless Being they really are.

existence: that which is being.

experience: the undergoing of things generally, be they internal events—such as sensations, emotions, feelings, thoughts or intuitions—or external events; the process of encountering Being through its manifestations; the totality of your perceived and remembered encounters with Being.

experience of Being: consciously encountering Being; being conscious.

Expert In Life: an approach to living based on consciously and expertly utilizing your faculties toward the fulfillment of your life's meaning and the realization of your potential.

faculties: your instruments—
body, senses, mind, emotions,
feelings, intellect and
intuition—for experiencing
and expressing.

false guide: a person who:
promises to overcome your
resistances without you
having to do any of the work;
appeals to ego, to the sense of
separateness and need; plays
upon weaknesses such as low
self-regard and consequent
fear, anxiety and depression;
plays upon the patterns,
weaknesses, by which people
are bound.

false modesty: attitude that 'all is
interconnected except for little
me,' founded on the mistaken
perception of isolation rooted
in relating to oneself as ego.

falsity: untruth; not reality.

feeling: a perceptive state; a
subtle, internal experience
in relation to inner or outer
conditions.

focus: to draw the attentiveness of
your faculties to yourself.

frustration: the painful feeling
experienced as a result of
dwelling in a state contrary
to who you really are and
what you really want; the
consequence of living in
opposition to yourself.

fulfillment: the state resulting
from the experience of your
infinite interconnectedness in
which you realize that you are
all and have all; the cessation
of need.

guide: teacher on the spiritual
path.

habit: automatic behavior patterns
based on repetition, often
opposed to conscious choice.

harmlessness: ethical and moral
behavior predicated upon
your understanding of your
intimate interconnectedness
with all creations; not
harming creatures large and
small in the knowledge they
are all manifestations of the
Being that we all are.

health: fully balanced system of
forces.

I-Amness: sense of 'I am,' free
of the limiting adjuncts; self-
recognition; Being.

identity: the irreducible and
permanent factor without
which you could not be; who
you are essentially.

illusion: false experience; not
reality; regarding things as
other than they are.

implicit covenant: absolute
agreement; inherent promise.

indweller: the one in the center
who is aware of Self.

inertia: the tendency to continue in the same state unless another and greater force causes a change; a powerful and persistent tendency that can resist growth.

initiate: one who has received initiation.

initiation: the most powerful, honest and interconnected relationship with a real teacher; relationship with the ultimate reality, with real Self; relationship with a guide that can ensure the aspirant's success on the path to the realization of highest potential.

initiation vow: commitment to always be true to your guide, to always be true to who you really are.

inner court: the very center of the royal realm, the ultimate evolutionary goal.

Inner Knower: the serene honest voice within that guides you with its utterly reliable truth.

inspiration: response to the urgings of the essence, the spirit that you are; a powerful motivating force; impetus to realize Self.

integrity: being true to reality, to who you are and to your knowledge and your determination.

intellect: the power of knowing that includes the ability to extrapolate and reason.

interconnectedness: unrestricted union.

intuition: your subtle ability of spontaneous cognition without evident rational thought or sensory experience.

knowledge: to have cognition of any facet of reality as a result of direct experience.

learning: the life process of acknowledging and integrating experience of reality.

love: unconditional acceptance; the harmonious realization of fundamental essence shared.

manifestation: the expression of Being.

meditation: the unalloyed experience of Being, including the knowledge of what Being is, with clarity and continuity, without distraction and at will.

mind: the faculty that gathers input from the other faculties and coordinates and reflects it for your experience.

negative: that which conceals, obscures or distorts the experience of real Being; that which is ultimately disadvantageous.

non-being: illusion, falsity, ego.

non-self: illusion, falsity, ego.

objects: phenomena caused by the coming and going of atoms creating the appearance of material of shape and weight.

path (evolutionary, spiritual): the way to fulfillment in reality; the way to the highest level of consciousness in which we experience ourselves continuously and in reality as the imperishable, all-pervasive, conscious power of Being.

perfect action: any action performed in consciousness of real Self; action without attachment to results, free of the binding consequences of action, the cycles of action and reaction that can occupy your energies endlessly.

phenomena: momentary events; the passing.

point of knowledge: words that guide you on the path to fulfillment through living according to your true identity and thereby freeing yourself from the self-imposed limitations that curtail human lives.

positive: that which reveals and contributes to the experience of real Being; that which is ultimately advantageous.

potential (human): the full capability of all our faculties; living in the full continuous consciousness of infinite Being.

power of Being: the power or energy that gives everything the ability to be; the substance of all that is.

practical: actually works toward accomplishing the goal.

practice: the repeated, intelligent use of a faculty by will.

pride: a distorted opinion of one's worth in an attempt to compensate for feelings of insecurity, rooted in ego.

procrastination: the act of indefinitely delaying the fulfillment of your intentions.

rationalization: lying to yourself.

reality: that which is, independent of circumstance, condition, time and space; the underlying absolute.

realize: making real your relationship to reality by living it.

resistance: that which opposes change; that which keeps you from realizing true Self.

responsibility: the ability to respond.

restraint: purposeful practice of behaviors that contradict the patterns of your past that bind you to suffering and pain.

royal realm: the state in which you experience illumination and fulfillment; reality.

sage: one who experiences and lives the transcendent and ultimate reality.

self: limited ego concept.

Self: your unchanging identity; that which you are essentially; the irreducible substance without which you could not be; infinite Being.

self-empowerment: acting in the experience and expression of real Self.

self-observant: having your observing powers, your faculties, focused upon the Being you are; causing every one of your faculties to live with great attentiveness to the all-inclusive Self.

Self-realization: knowledge of Self that is actualized by living, experiencing and expressing it; being congruent with knowledge of Self and thus freed from identification with the limiting ego construct.

senses: the perceptive capabilities by which you relate to the material realm: taste, smell, hearing, sight and touch.

separate agency: sense of a separate agent of action, separate doer; a false perception, ego sense.

service (selfless, egoless): acting in the consciousness of interconnectedness; action without attachment to the results or desire for rewards.

Silent Observer: unattached witness to all events, external and internal.

soul: essence, spirit.

spirit: the essence; the true intent or meaning of something.

student: limitless Being in the guise of separateness who is being guided by limitless Being into the experience of interconnectedness.

substance: that which stands under; the real or essential.

suffering: the result of ignorance regarding, or disregard of, your true Self.

transcendent: beyond the limits and qualifications of time and space.

transformation: permanent change to a higher level.

truth: that which unequivocally is.

ultimate practicality: living according to your true identity.

unattachment: not involving yourself in particulars at the expense of your involvement in the infinite wholeness.

unitive state: self-knowing oneness, Being experienced in clarity, spontaneously, from moment to moment without end; being in the experience of complete devotion to, and absorption in, infinite Being.

universal: all-inclusive; without limit or exception.

unreality: that which is not; the momentary; illusion.

vibratory modes: the modes of vibration that compose all manifestation of Being: active, static and dynamically balanced.

wanderer: human representative, both masculine and feminine.

will: the power by which you implement your choices.

wisdom: knowledge gained by experience of reality continuously applied to your behaviors and actions.

Yoga: the cessation of the modifications of the mind; the experience of the unitive state; the multi-faceted discipline and approach of realizing the unitive state.

PHOTOGRAPH CAPTIONS
Photographs by Erhard Vogel

Front Cover and Page ix
Shah's Audience Hall
India 1983

Page 25
Udaipur Tower
India 2010

Page xi
Cactus Flower
Nataraja Ashram 2008

Page 57
Erhard Meditating in Cave
India 1979
Photographer: Anon.

Page xv
Buddha
Nataraja Ashram 2009

Page 135
A Wave
Pacific Ocean 2010

Page xvii
Goats through Arch
India 2010

Page 219
Ashram Visitor
Nataraja Ashram 2012

Page 1
View from Cave
India 1979

Page 245
Udaipur Fountain
India 2010

Page 5
Gates with Wanderer
India 2010

Back Cover
Shah's Audience Hall
India 2010

ABOUT THE AUTHOR

Erhard Vogel, PhD, is recognized as one of the foremost meditation and Self-realization teachers in the world. Born in war-torn Germany, Dr. Vogel immigrated to the United States at age fourteen. He graduated from the Pratt Institute of Design in New York, and at an early age rose to a respected position in a world-renowned architectural firm. At thirty-one, he set aside a brilliant career in architecture to devote himself to the service of humanity.

For four years Erhard, as he likes to be called by his students, traveled the globe on foot. He lived in the Middle East, India and China, thoroughly researching the ways in which people of different cultures seek fulfillment. He saw the underlying need in everyone to fulfill their potential.

Erhard returned home to address the problems and aspirations of our contemporary society with his teachings. Following a lecture tour spanning the United States, Europe and Canada, he came to San Diego and founded the Nataraja Yoga Ashram, a not-for-profit organization.

Erhard's teachings are a unique combination of time-tested wisdom and pragmatic methods. His fundamental, systematic approach is based upon sound psychological, physiological and spiritual principles that make meditation and Self-realization practical and attainable.

A true guide—one who cultivates positive experiences of reality in students to have them live true to themselves—Erhard teaches not from books nor from other people's ideas, but out of his own profound life experience. Through his depth of knowledge he is able to inspire and gently guide sincere students to the experience of their limitless potential. With unconditional acceptance and unwavering respect for the Being they are, he inspires his students to recognize the real Self and to treat themselves with trust and kindness.

Since 1969, Erhard has taught tens of thousands of students throughout the world. He travels regularly to India and teaches among the sages in the Himalayas, where he is recognized as a Master Teacher. He has authored three additional books, *Self-healing Through the Awareness of Being, Journey Into Your Center* and *A Dialogue With Death The Teacher Of Life: An Ancient Story For The Modern World,* as well as numerous audio recordings, and magazine and newspaper articles. Erhard currently offers courses on site and online through the Nataraja Meditation and Yoga Center in San Diego, California.

ABOUT THE NATARAJA YOGA ASHRAM

The Nataraja Yoga Ashram is an organization for Self-realization. Established by Dr. Erhard Vogel in 1974 in San Diego, California, as a not-for-profit social service organization, the Nataraja Yoga Ashram provides in-depth experiential teachings of expert ways to lead a fulfilling and successful life that is realistically directed toward the attainment of Self-realization in this lifetime.

Through a wide array of on-site as well as worldwide Internet programs and services, the Nataraja Yoga Ashram is dedicated to promoting the physiological, psychological and spiritual welfare of the human being.

The Expert In Life™ Program was developed by Dr. Vogel over a lifetime of direct experience to provide the direct means by which to live in the state of Self-realization: fully self-aware and self-accepting, free from limitation, in deep inner peace and quietly balanced joy.

The Expert In Life Program is a graduated group process centered around pro-active life application practices and strengthened by a shared commitment to success. It is the objective of the Expert In Life program to empower students to become so expert at understanding, fine-tuning and strengthening their faculties that they can harmoniously integrate and skillfully apply them toward fulfillment.

AUDIO PUBLICATIONS BY ERHARD VOGEL

The Cave Meditation This powerful meditation on CD comes to you from the direct experience of world-renowned Meditation Master, Erhard Vogel, who dwelled in a Himalayan cave and taught among the sages of the Himalayas. Allow yourself to be guided into a state of clear, focused consciousness in which all aspects of you rest in effortless balance in your center, reflecting the infinity of Being that you are.
Available on Amazon.com.

The Stress Release Response: 7 Steps to Triumph Over Stress This guided experience on CD contains a set of steps by which you can dependably free yourself from stress and its harmful effects—at a moment's notice and at will. Dr. Vogel has taught tens of thousands of students from many parts of the world and walks of life to effectively reduce anxiety and stress, including members of such high-stress professions as hospice workers, doctors, lawyers, police officers, teachers and mothers. The Stress Release Response™, which he developed in the 1970s to answer an unmet need, has proven to be among the most beneficial means of coping with stress, yielding predictably positive results. Available on Amazon.com.

Guided Meditation for Beginners This meditation provides an inspiring and enjoyable experience in which you will learn the fundamental steps necessary for meditation, and cultivate your ability to relax at will, focus your mind, and know yourself and your potential on the deepest level.

Centering In this meditation you are guided in a unique and powerfully effective method of making the state of clear and centered consciousness directly available. Anyone who sincerely implements the step-by-step suggestions will create an inner state that is vibrant and attentive as well as deeply relaxed, thus overcoming internal struggles, mental distraction and the 'zoned-out' state that is often mistaken for meditation.

Feelings and Emotions Human experiences, including our feelings and emotions, are richly varied. However, we habitually repress our feelings because we fear they would overwhelm us. With this guided experience you will relate to your emotions with acceptance and become deeply in touch with your feelings. With repeated listening, you will open to ever subtler levels and no longer experience your feelings as distractions, but as enriching aspects of your Self-experience.

The Healing Power of Love Imagine having everything about you in such a pure, clear and luminous state that your deepest insights and inner light shine forth in unrestricted strength. With this meditation, you will guide your faculties to harmonious union and thereby develop a powerful, peaceful love of yourself that creates healing from the physical to the deepest levels.

The Silent Observer Learn to guide your faculties into a calm, clear and balanced state in which you experience yourself as the unattached witness to all events, external and internal. You attain a level of perception and judgment far subtler and more lucid than your ordinary mental processes allow. The relief and freedom gained by becoming skilled at maintaining the Silent Observer state is a significant aid to anyone who wants a life of empowerment and peace.

Yoga For Life Erhard instructs you with clear, detailed description through a wide variety of yoga postures in two hour-long classes. Whether you are a beginner or advanced, you will find it easy to give yourself your own rejuvenating classes at home. This will benefit you on all levels: developing flexibility and strength, deeply calming and centering the mind, creating a state of balance emotionally and on every level. You will use these recordings for years to come, growing ever healthier and more powerful in your concentration.

Advanced Breathing Techniques and the Breath Meditation: This set of two recordings guides you through: 1 the super-oxygenation and alternate nostril breathing techniques, or *pranayama*, which you can employ to dramatically increase your clarity, vitality and concentration, as well as balance and fine-tune your nervous system; and 2 the *Breath Meditation*, a guided experience in harmonious breathing requisite to meditation, in which this natural process becomes deeply significant and strengthens your experience of Being.

For more information visit yogameditationnataraja.org

Made in the USA
Las Vegas, NV
14 April 2022

47459616R00184